English
Weapons &
Warfare
449~1660

English Weapons & Warfare 449-1660

A.V.B. Norman and Don Pottinger

DORSET PRESS
NEW YORK

This edition published by Dorset Press, a division of Marboro
Books Corporation, by arrangement with Arms and Armour Press
1985 Dorset Press

Originally published in 1966, under the title *Warrior to Soldier
449-1660,* by Weidenfeld and Nicholson (Educational) Limited,
and as *A History of War and Weapons 449 to 1660* in the U.S.A.
by Thomas Y. Crowell Company.

ISBN 0-88029-44-7
(Formerly ISBN 0-85368-472-3)

Printed in the United States of America

1 2 3 4 5 6 7 8 9 10

To Jemma, Jaspar and Jocelyn

Contents

Contents by Subjects

T TACTICS AND STRATEGY

CASTLES AND CANNONS

Preface

THE period covered by this book begins at the traditional date of the Anglo-Saxon invasion and ends with the foundation of the Standing Army by Charles II. There is no real link with military organisation before 449, and in 1660 the modern British Army had its beginning. Our aim has been to describe briefly the organisation and equipment of the fighting man, his tactics and fortifications, within this period, but we are very aware that in a book of this sort generalisation and over-simplification are unavoidable and that much that we would like to have said has had to be left out.

We have tried to avoid using too many technical names and at the same time tried to avoid jargon altogether. For instance, we have used 'gown' in place of the more usual 'surcoat', since the latter seems to have referred to a purely civilian garment at the time, while the former was used for both civilian and military clothing.

The book is divided into chapters in the normal way, but is also arranged in four parallel streams which can be read separately if the reader wishes. These cover – 1. Organisation, including pay and training, indicated by an 0 in the top corner of the page or in the margin; 2. Arms and Armour, similarly indicated by a † ; 3. Tactics and Strategy, indicated by a T ; 4. Castles and Cannons, indicated by a ♖ .

This does not profess to be a work of research and we would like to acknowledge our debt to the following books: C. Blair, *European*

Preface

Armour, circa 1066 to circa 1700, London, 1958, and *European and American Arms, c.1100–1850*, London, 1962; R. A. Brown, *English Castles*, London, 1962; A. H. Burne, *The Crécy War*, London, 1955, and *The Agincourt War*, London, 1956; C. G. Cruickshank, *Elizabeth's Army*, Oxford, 1946; C. H. Frith, *Cromwell's Army*, London, 1962; J. Hewitt, *Ancient Armour and Weapons in Europe* 3 vols., London, 1855–60; C. W. Hollister, *Anglo-Saxon Military Institutions on the Eve of the Norman Conquest*, Oxford, 1962, and *The Military Organization of Norman England*, Oxford, 1965; R. E. Oakeshott, *The Sword in the Age of Chivalry*, London, 1964; C. W. C. Oman, *A History of the Art of War in the Middle Ages*, 2 vols., London, 1924, and *A History of the Art of War in the Sixteenth Century*, London, 1937; B. H. St. J. O'Neil, *Castles and Cannons*, Oxford, 1960.

Finally we would like to express our especial gratitude to Mr C. Blair, MA, FSA, of the Victoria and Albert Museum for his assistance and advice, and for reading the manuscript of this book with a firmly critical eye.

Vesey Norman and Don Pottinger

English
Weapons &
Warfare
449~1660

Chapter One

The Invaders

THE SAXON WARRIOR

The heathen Anglo-Saxon warrior was fanatically devoted to fighting and thought of it as by far the most important thing in life. He believed that his mighty deeds in battle were his hope of eternity. 'Let him who can, achieve glory before he die that will be best for the lifeless warrior afterwards,' says the Saxon poet. The young warrior joined the war-band of the most successful and experienced warrior he could find and followed him devotedly, eager for the fighting, the booty, and above all the glory and renown that such a leader must surely bring. There was no tribal link between lord and warrior, and famous chiefs were followed by men of many tribes.

War-bands of these Angle and Saxon warriors came to Britain in the fifth century, some as mercenary soldiers hired to fight the Pictish and Irish raiders, some as raiders themselves. A few settled down and lived peacefully alongside the Britons, as at York; others massacred and burnt all before them.

Fierce warriors, such as these, often fought among themselves too, and their lord was expected to avenge the death of one of his men with the blood of the slayer, or with a payment, called the *wergild*, to the dead man's lord and next-of-kin, extracted from the slayer. The lord of the war-band was expected to be generous to his warriors, providing them with gold rings, horses, arms and armour, protection in their quarrels, and food and wine in his hall. In exchange, the men gave their loyalty to death and beyond, for if by chance their lord should be killed before them, they were bound by honour to avenge him. Those that fled would be called *nithing*, coward, and live out their lives dishonoured. At the battle of Maldon in 991, when Earl Brythnoth fell, his followers fought doubly hard in order to die beside him or to avenge him.

On the death of a man, unless in battle, the lord's gifts to him were returned symbolically by a due called 'heriot'. Saxon wills mention heriots of swords, horses, harness, spears, shields and armour. In the Middle Ages heriot became the equivalent of modern death duties: it was charged on the belongings of a dead man and no longer bore any relationship to its literal meaning of 'war gear'.

The ordinary Saxon warrior wore only civilian clothes. He was usually armed with a spear and sometimes with a sword or axe and carried a round shield. The spear-heads and iron shield-bosses are often found today when Saxon graves are excavated; the wooden parts have, of course, all rotted away. Swords and axes are rare, and armour rarer still. The Saxon war leaders wore a defensive shirt, called a 'byrnie', made of many small interlinked iron rings – the type of armour known as mail. Their poets called them the 'ring-woven corslets' and 'the woven breast-net'. They were usually waist-length but sometimes reached down to mid-thigh. The sleeves were always short.

The Saxon warrior prized his sword very highly. It was often handed down from father to son, and especially mentioned in the will of the dead man, like the sword which had belonged to King Offa (died 796) left by the eleventh-century Prince Athelstan to his brother. The Saxon poets spoke of them as 'the ancient heir-loom' and the warrior believed that his sword possessed some of the 'luck', courage and prowess of its former owner. A sword given by King Edmund to a man called Ælfgar was valued at 120 man-cuses of gold – equivalent to 120 oxen or fifteen male slaves – and *Beowulf* frequently refers to gold-hilted swords. 'Lucky' swords or richly mounted ones were usually too precious to bury with their

Saxon warrior

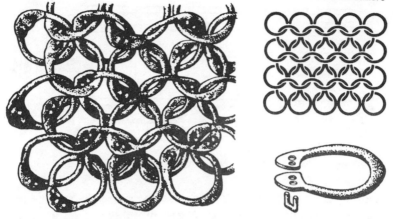

A piece of mail, with diagrams of construction

dead owners unless they were very great warriors, but one was placed in the memorial ship of an East Anglian king of the mid-seventh century buried at Sutton-Hoo in Suffolk, and is now in the British Museum. The hilt and belt were decorated with gold and cut and polished garnets set in a pattern of steps and quatrefoils.

The earlier Saxon swords have straight, two-edged blades, about thirty-three inches long, of steel, with very little taper and rather round points. A shallow groove, called the 'fuller', ran almost the full length of the blade on both sides. This was not a gutter for blood as is so often said but was to lighten the blade without weakening it. The last few inches of the blade at the hand end, called the 'tang', are made narrower and pass through a wooden or horn grip, sometimes covered with precious metal or wire. In front of the grip, a short cross-bar acted as a guard, although, in the early examples, this was of horn or other perishable material so that it was probably intended merely to prevent the hand slipping down on to the blade. At the other end of the grip, to protect the hand from the sharp end of the tang, a knob known as the 'pommel' was fitted. In the early Saxon period this

15

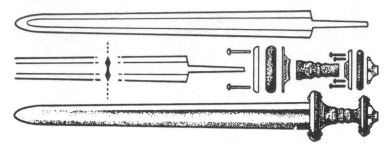

Early Saxon sword, with diagram of construction

took several forms but the commonest was a straight bar like the hand-guard, with a cocked-hat-shaped protuberance on it on the opposite side to the grip.

The scabbard was formed of two thin boards shaped to each side of the blade, covered in leather to hold them together, mounted in iron or precious metal, and sometimes lined with sheep's fleece. The grease of the fleece would help to keep the blade from rusting. The sword-belt, often gold-mounted and jewelled, was worn rather loosely round the waist so that the sword hung on the left hip, or was occasionally slung over the right shoulder.

Many highly prized swords were given names, such as Beowulf's *Naegling*, and were traditionally made by the mythical smith Weland, while many later blades are signed by their actual makers, such as Ingelrii and Ulfberht.

Apart from the great gold-covered helmet from Sutton-Hoo which was old when it was buried and probably came from Sweden, only one of the helmets worn by the Saxon leaders has come down to us. It comes from a burial mound at Benty Grange in Derbyshire and consists of a steel frame formerly filled with horn plates. On top stands a bronze boar decorated with pieces of silver cut from an old Roman vessel. The eyes are garnets, and it was perhaps at one time enamelled all over. This is the emblem of the ancient Saxon goddess Frig (who gave her name to Friday),

Saxon sword-belt

16

Saxon helmet excavated from a grave at Benty Grange, Derbyshire
(Sheffield Museum)

which the Saxon warrior believed would protect him. Helmets
adorned with boars are mentioned in *Beowulf* as being made by the
smiths of old so that no blade could pierce them. Here the luck of
the ancient gods has been strengthened by the symbol of the newer
Christ, for on the nose-guard is a silver crucifix.

The Saxon spear, the weapon of their god Woden, was used
both for stabbing and for casting like a javelin. It had a long steel
leaf-shaped head with a socket to fit over the seven-foot ash staff.
Two wings usually sprang from the base of the blade. As this type
of spear was also used for hunting wild boar, the wings were
perhaps intended to prevent the onrush of the impaled beast. The
bottom of the shaft was also steel-mounted.

Saxon spear

17

Saxon spear head

The bows used by the Saxons for hunting and war were about four- to five-feet long. Although they have all rotted away long ago, traces of them, together with a few arrowheads, are sometimes found in the soil of graves. They are mentioned in poems of the time and illustrated in manuscripts and carvings.

The Bayeux Tapestry, which illustrates the Battle of Hastings, shows Saxons armed with clubs, some of which are being thrown. One of the chroniclers of the battle speaks of stones tied to sticks being hurled, and small throwing axes were also used.

The wooden shield was round and probably sometimes convex, covered in leather and reinforced with a metal rim and bands. It was held by means of a handgrip inside the metal boss. The thin limewood discs would be easy to manœuvre in order to parry a blow.

Saxon bow

0 THE DANISH RAIDERS

The fierce and bloody Danish raiders of the ninth century, unleashed by the collapse of strong government in their own country, fell on an England divided into a number of warring kingdoms but dotted with rich and undefended monasteries and churches. By the middle of the century armies consisting of as many as 350 ships' companies were landing and even wintering in stockaded camps. Their ships gave them mobility: if the Saxons were too strong for them at one point, they could sail swiftly away and land again somewhere else where the natives were quite unprepared.

These men were only raiders, planning to return to Denmark

Reconstruction of the Sutton-Hoo shield; front, back, and side views
(British Museum)

laden with booty. The great Danish army which ravaged England
in the 'sixties and 'seventies was a different matter; it stayed for
thirteen years, moving camp frequently, riding across the country
at great speed on stolen horses, and capturing even cities like York
and London. It was finally defeated by Alfred at Edington in
878 after routing him again and again, and nearly capturing all
England. The Danes held the north-east and strongly influenced
the development of the legal and naval future of England. More
importantly, from our point of view, they introduced new weapons
and caused new developments in English tactics.

The Danish sword had a more tapering point which made it
lighter near the top and therefore easier to wield. It could be used
both to cut and to stab. The guard was usually a little longer than

Danish sword

Danish axe found at Mammen in Jutland

on the Saxon sword and was curved towards the blade. The pommel was usually of tea-cosy shape or of similar form but built up of lobes. A favourite Danish weapon was the battle-axe, the head of which had a large trumpet-shaped blade and was mounted on an ash handle long enough to be used in both hands.

THE SAXON ARMY

The Danish invaders were full-time warriors, living off the country and able to give their whole attention to fighting. The Saxons, on the other hand, were by now farmers and administrators as well as warriors. Although it is probable that originally the army could be called out for an unlimited period, in reality the men could not serve indefinitely since their crops and jobs required their presence. Agriculture, in particular, would soon have come to a standstill if neglected too long, and that would have meant starvation for everyone.

King Alfred overcame this difficulty by organising his forces so that only half would be out at any one time, while the rest stayed at home to mind the crops and run the country. Thus he could plan long campaigns, knowing that when the first part of the army had completed its service and wanted to go home, a second force would be ready to replace it. The Danish armies had no such relief and could be worn down by keeping them constantly in action. Alfred's small fleet of sixty-oared ships was probably intended more to give his forces the same mobility along the coast as the Danes than to fight them at sea. An army could move much faster by sea along the coast than over the almost roadless wastes of Saxon England.

One of the three services owed by every freeman to the King was that of building fortifications, and the much earlier Offa's Dyke dividing Mercia from Wales must have been built by this method. Alfred, probably with the example of the Danish fortified camps in front of him, began the founding of a system of burghs, or walled towns, all over Wessex and Mercia, which was continued by his successors as they slowly conquered the Danelaw. The walls were maintained and manned by the men of the surrounding countryside. These fortresses formed rallying points for the Saxons and helped to counteract the mobility of the Danes by providing a strong refuge against surprise attacks.

By the time of the Norman invasion the Saxon army was highly organised and well armed. It now consisted of three groups. First, there was the King's personal bodyguard, the 'housecarles'. This consisted of well-trained, heavily armed, professional soldiers living at the court and receiving the King's pay. They are said to have been raised by the Danish King Cnut in about 1018 on the model of the *Jómsvikings* of his grandfather, Harold Bluetooth of Denmark. Earlier English kings had certainly had paid bodyguards, a development from the war-band of early times: the housecarles perhaps only differed from these in being organised as a fraternity with a strict code of rules, and in meeting as judges on their own members. The housecarles were paid for by special tax, called the Army Tax. Both English and Danes served in their ranks but their characteristic weapon was the great Danish axe with the heavy curved blade. By the time of Hastings the great earls had their own bodyguards of housecarles, and those of Harold's brothers, the Earls Gyrth and Leofwine, must have

Anglo-Danish axe

21

fought in that battle beside their lords.

The second part of the Saxon army consisted of those who owed military service to the King because of their estates. From early Saxon times England appears to have been divided up for purposes of military service and taxation into areas known as 'hides', probably the measure of land originally required to maintain one family.

By the end of the Saxon period each area of five hides was expected to provide an armed warrior wearing helmet and byrnie. Estates of five hides in Domesday Book are usually held by thegns, and the cheorl who throve so that he acquired five hides could become a thegn. Men of this class served in person.

Where the five hides were held by more than one man, they banded together to equip one of their number with helmet and byrnie and provisions for two months, or four shillings for each hide. A similar system also covered the Danelaw. From this it will be seen that armour must now have become much more common than before.

This part of the army would include the followings of the greater thegns, who held many times five hides of land. They provided their quotas by the same method, or from their own bodyguards, or by means of special tenants holding land in return for military service.

Both these parts of the army are described by the *Anglo-Saxon Chronicle* as riding to battle and in some cases actually fighting on horseback. At Hastings, the Saxons all fought on foot, possibly because only part of the army was present and it was thought essential to fight a defensive action.

It is these two groups which formed the trained and manageable part of the army. In times of emergency the King could call upon the service of every freeman, and these formed the third and largest group of the Saxon army. From the earliest times all freemen owed the King three services: the construction of fortifications, bridge-building, and military service. The last was rarely enforced except for local defence, the force in each county serving only within that shire or its immediate neighbours. It was not mounted and was only lightly armed. It is probably the Sussex men of this class who are shown as archers and clubmen in the Bayeux Tapestry.

The King himself usually led important expeditions, and the forces of the shire were at first led by the King's deputy, the Ealdorman, but, in the absence of the King, the Ealdorman or even a bishop might lead the whole army. In later Saxon times, when the Ealdorman was replaced by the Earl, the latter usually led the forces of several shires, which would each be commanded under him by its own shire-reeve. Of the smaller divisions of the army very little is known but, in at least one case, all the soldiers from the estates of a particular bishop served as a unit within the army.

By the time of the Conquest the period of service seems to have been for two months at a stretch.

The fighting formation of the Saxons was called, poetically, the 'shield wall'. The mail-clad warriors – the thegns and the representatives of five hides – would have formed the centre of the army around the King and the dragon banner of Saxon England. Their round shields were held before them to ward off arrows and spears. The flanks of the army would have been formed of the lightly armed forces of the shire. The battle began with the hurling of spears and insults and a shower of arrows. When the armies closed, the fighting consisted of exchanging blows which would, if possible, be avoided by leaping clear or by catching them on the shield. This type of fencing means that the shields cannot have been interlocked, as is sometimes suggested, and that 'shield wall' is poetical rather than truly descriptive. When the axe was used in both hands no doubt the shield was slung over the shoulder. At Hastings the Saxons encouraged each other by cries of 'Holy Cross' and, as the fighting grew harder and the day grimmer, by shouting 'Out, out'.

Hastings was an extremely hard-fought battle, in spite of the fact that the Saxon army cannot have been in the best of condition. It had just marched the full length of England after fighting a major battle, nineteen days earlier, against the Danes under Hardrada, one of the greatest warriors of his age. There had been too short a time for summonses to reach reinforcements and for them to join the army. Duke William is said to have criticised the Saxons for their poor archery; probably the bowmen, who had apparently done well at Stamford Bridge, were not with the army, having fallen behind on the forced march from the north.

The contemporary reputation of the Saxons can be gauged by William of Normandy's reluctance to leave the area of his bridge-head at Pevensey from which he would be able to beat a retreat if defeated. In fact there were several moments in the day when it looked as if the Norman ranks might break.

Late Saxon sword

THE NORMAN SYSTEM

Two tasks awaited the Conqueror after defeating the Saxon army in the field, capturing the main town, London, and being accepted by the Witan, the advisory council of the Saxon kings. These were the subjugation of the English and the settlement of his own followers in such a way that the worst evils of the feudal system of the Continent – overpowerful subjects and private wars between barons – were avoided.

Before describing how the Conqueror organised the military forces of his new country, something must be said about how the feudal system developed.

At a time when Dane and Magyar were raiding the outposts of the Frankish Empire and yearly penetrating deeper, the collapse of the central power of the Empire under Charlemagne's successors left defence and administration in the hands of the Counts, the Imperial deputies. With the Emperor far away, and powerless in any case, no one else could organise the resistance to the raiders.

The mailed horsemen and fortresses of the Counts slowly made raiding unprofitable, but not before the economic position of the freemen had been so depressed that they were forced to make themselves the dependants of the Counts, who by now were becoming hereditary. By the eleventh century a complex system of services and obligations had evolved. All land was regarded as belonging to the King under God. The tenants-in-chief, the greater nobles, held land from the King in return for stipulated military service. They, in turn, would sub-let to individuals who would serve in the quota of knights owed to the King. These tenants and sub-tenants had a duty to the peasants of administering justice in the courts and of defending them in return for agricultural work and payment in food and produce. The essence of the system was protection in return for service.

The Normans had completely absorbed this system from their neighbours and, as we shall see, did much to perfect it.

Of the 5,000 or so knights who followed Duke William to England less than half were his Norman tenants; the majority were Flemings, Aquitanians, or Frenchmen seeking their fortunes in this rich island. Even his own tenants refused to follow him as such and were only induced to set out by promises of conquered lands. William portioned out the land in a strict system, each of about 200 great nobles receiving a large number of manors scattered over the country in return for the service of five, or multiples of five, knights. These manors were probably not scattered intentionally in order to prevent any one noble owning a single large block of land which might make it easy for him to revolt there, although it had this effect. The King could only distribute a little land at a time since the Conquest was only completed bit by bit; often he gave an individual baron the lands held by a single Saxon before the Conquest, and these were frequently scattered up and down the country. The Church also held its land in return for the service of some 800 knights.

The King did not stipulate how the tenants-in-chief were to produce their military quotas. Some hired knights, when the King required them, from among the many landless younger sons, trained from childhood to warfare, seeking their fortunes, and hoping by serving some magnate in war to receive a knight's fee of their own. Others provided them from among the knights of their own households, normally employed to guard their castles or escort them on the long journeys across England and Normandy from one manor to another. Finally, as the Saxons began to settle down and large bodies of household knights became less essential, the great majority sub-let their land to lesser barons or to individual knights in return for the necessary military service.

The tenant-in-chief received his land from the King at a ceremony in which, kneeling at his feet and placing his hands within the King's, he swore to keep faith with the King and serve him always, and none other except God. The lesser barons and knights received their land at a similar ceremony in which they swore to be faithful to the lord who was giving them the land, excepting only their duty to God and the King. Late in his reign the Conqueror decided that this type of oath was insufficient to prevent the tenants of a great lord from serving against the King. In order to bind them to him more closely, an oath of personal fealty to him was taken at Salisbury in 1086 by, or on behalf of, all land-holders of any account, regardless of who their immediate overlord might be. Since he was making a total reorganisation William could enforce uniformity on his tenants. This same form of military service by round numbers of fully armed knights was demanded of all. Varying periods of service by half-armed knights, common on the Continent, were unknown in England.

In addition to the feudal part of the army, all the Norman and Angevin kings employed large bodies of mercenary soldiers, usually from Brittany or Flanders. The Danegeld was still being levied and was used to pay these men.

NORMAN REORGANISATION

Apart from the necessity of preventing the Saxons from revolting, it was essential that they be incorporated into the organisation of the land. William was acclaimed by the Witan and crowned in the

Confessor's new abbey at Westminster, swearing to keep Edward's laws. To make himself appear as the true heir of the Saxon kings, not only by conquest but by legal descent, he made every effort to give his succession continuity by employing many Englishmen, such as Archbishop Stigand and Earl Morcar of Northumbria, and by using all that was best of English institutions, such as the shire- and hundred-courts and the excellent Saxon coinage. Apart from anything else, these features of life were much better organised in Saxon England than in Normandy.

From our point of view, the most important of the Saxon institutions which the Conqueror continued to employ was the military organisation – the right to call upon every freeman to serve the King in war, the selective service by which one man served on behalf of and at the expense of others who stayed at home, and the summons of this force by means of a letter sent to the sheriff. This force, known as the shire levy, together with similar town levies, was used to augment the feudal army and, particularly, to act as a counterweight against overpowerful barons. Although William had forbidden private wars to his followers, they were fierce and bloody men unused to such restraint, and his own reign and that of his son were filled with baronial wars and revolts. In the great baronial risings, such as that of the Earls of Hereford and East Anglia, in 1075, Saxon thegns and freemen fought for the King alongside his loyal Norman feudatories. Even in the first years of the reign they were called out and fought against Harold's brothers in 1068 and against the last Danish invasions of 1069 and 1070. The Commander of the Saxons of Somerset fighting for the King in 1068 was a Saxon, Eadnoth, one of King Edward's household officers. The use of the English in this way was to be of great importance in the development of the Anglo-Norman feudal army of later periods.

THE NORMAN CASTLE

To strengthen himself against the danger of revolts by his powerful barons the King retained in his own hands the largest single group of manors. Both for this reason and to keep the English firmly in subjection he had many castles built, such as the great stone Tower just outside the east wall of London, to dominate the major towns.

The main strategic sites guarding the gateways for invaders, such as Durham, Chester, the Welsh Marches, and the vulnerable south-coast ports, were either occupied by the King or by his closest associates. A constable was appointed to command the garrison and was rewarded with an estate held by a right called 'castle guard'. The garrison, which in peacetime would be quite small, consisted of mercenaries or of knights doing their military service. Since the King's interests were the same as his tenants', he permitted them to build castles on their main manors in order to keep the Saxons in subjection.

To the average Saxon the castle must have been one of the most noticeable signs of the Conquest and, for the peasant, one of the most oppressive. Except for some three built by Norman favourites of Edward the Confessor, the private fortress was unknown in England before the Conquest. The typical Norman castle was a very simple affair and differed greatly from what the word brings to mind – stone walls and pointed towers. The Bayeux Tapestry illustrates the type of wooden palisade and small wooden tower, such as the Duke erected at Hastings as his headquarters. It consisted of an artificial mound of earth, known as the 'motte', surrounded by the ditch from which the mound was dug and topped by a tower or house within a palisade. This was connected by a movable bridge to a larger palisaded area, called the 'bailey', also surrounded by a ditch and rampart. Some castles of this type had

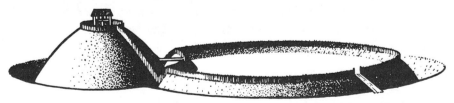

A motte and bailey castle

two baileys.

The motte tower was the refuge in time of trouble, while the bailey contained stables, storehouses, and the dwellings of the garrison and of the owner, if necessary. Probably only the larger towers were inhabited all the time. Once the earth had been allowed to settle, some of these mottes were topped with a stone tower, which they could not have supported when the earth was newly dug. In one case the earth was held from sliding down by an overall coating of clay. At Farnham Castle there was a stone tower inside the mound to support the weight of the tower which originally stood on top. Many hundreds of this type of castle must have existed all over the Islands: some 900 are still recognisable. The spreading of Norman influence took them to Ireland and to the north of Scotland. Many have been altered by later rebuilding; others remain as flat-topped, grassy mounds with the earthworks of the bailey. On some of them archaeologists have discovered the post holes of the palisade and tower.

NORMAN ARMS AND ARMOUR

Although the Normans were the descendants of the Norse war-band of Hrolf the Ganger and had only been settled in France for about 150 years, they had profited enormously by their contact with the French. Most important, they had learnt the art of cavalry warfare. By 993 the Norman contingent in the French army fought on horseback. The horse had carried the spearman into battle for many centuries but the spear had been used over-arm to thrust or had been thrown in the same way as the infantry spear. Now men began to tuck the spear under the arm, thus adding the weight of the rider and the speed of the horse to the force of the blow. This use of the spear probably developed because, due to the introduction of the stirrup, the rider sat more firmly in the saddle. Cavalry must be taught to manœuvre together as a body, and this cannot be done hurriedly at the beginning of a campaign. Thus we find that, unlike the Saxons, who, with the exception of the housecarles, served only in time of war,

Alternative methods of using lances

the Normans were called out in time of peace also.

The sword used by the Normans was similar to that of the Danes but usually had a rather longer, straighter guard above the hand, and the tea-cosy-shaped pommel was longer and more like a Brazil nut in form. It was carried in a scabbard on a wide loose waist-belt which the weight of the sword pulled down low over the left hip. The belt was buckled or knotted at the front and was occasionally worn under the hauberk, presumably to prevent it being cut. In this case the sword hilt emerged from a slit in the side of the hauberk.

Norman sword

Only with the greatest difficulty can even the best cavalry break steady and disciplined infantry who are in a position to receive them. The housecarles behind their shields would not have broken before William's knights if gaps had not been made in the shield wall by the Norman archers. Apparently, William's infantry was mainly composed of archers armed with shortbows drawn to the breast, and it was their employment which finally broke the resistance of the English and allowed the cavalry to overrun their position.

The Bayeux Tapestry shows the archers unarmoured, except for one man who was possibly intended to be a captain. The arrows were carried in an open-ended box, called a 'quiver', worn either over the shoulder or slung on the waist-belt. Contemporary descriptions show that many crossbowmen were present as well.

Norman archer

30

The crossbow consisted of a bow mounted at right angles to a straight stock. The bowstring was held in the spanned position by a catch on the stock. The arrow, or 'quarrel' as it was called, was placed in a groove on top of the stock in front of the cord. The bow was discharged by holding the stock against the cheek and releasing the catch which held back the string.

The armour of the Normans differed very little from that of the Saxons. Their mail shirt, which they called the 'hauberk', was usually knee-length and slit up to the fork of the legs so that the skirts could hang down on either side of the saddle. Most illustrations show a tight-fitting mail hood made in one with the shirt. Some hauberks were still used without hoods or were worn with what may have been cloth or leather hoods. A few of the leaders in the Bayeux Tapestry have cuff-length mail sleeves and mail hosen[1] worn under the hauberk, but these were rare. The hauberk was worn over a long garment rather like a nightshirt which can

[1] See p. 45.

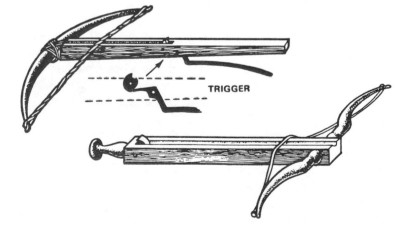

TRIGGER

Above, Norman crossbow   *Below,* Late Roman crossbow

Norman armour; from the Bayeux Tapestry

have given little protection against the weight and rubbing of the mail. One feature observed only in the Bayeux Tapestry and in two manuscripts is a rectangle on the breast, outlined in colour and apparently sometimes with laces or ties hanging from the corners. No one knows for certain what this was but it may represent an additional layer of mail or an extra reinforce of some sort over the breast, or it may have been the flap which closed the neck opening.

The helmet was worn alone or over the mail hood. That of St Wenceslaus of Bohemia (Good King Wenceslaus of the carol) has survived. The conical steel skull is made in one piece, and a rim with a separate bar to protect the nose is riveted on and inlaid with a crucifix in silver. Some nose-guards must have been quite wide, since we are told that at Hastings Duke William had to raise his helmet so that his men could recognise him when the cry went up that he had fallen. Some helmets of this type had a similar guard

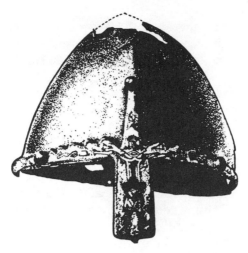

Helmet of St. Wenceslaus (died 935); (Prague Cathedral)

hanging down the back of the neck. Many illustrations show helmets apparently made up of segments with bars covering the
joints and with a rim to reinforce the lower edge.

The mounted man is particularly vulnerable down the left side.

Norman shields

33

He can protect his right side with his sword but the left side must be covered by his shield, and for this purpose a long shield is better than a round one. In consequence a long kite-shaped shield was developed which covered the body and most of the left leg. It consisted of wood, probably covered with leather and bound with steel bands, usually with a boss in the centre of the upper part. The left forearm passed through a square of straps at the back of the shield, and the hand grasped a handgrip. There was also a long strap, called the 'guige', which went round the neck over the right shoulder and supported the shield when not in use and took part of its weight from the left arm in action. The surface of the shield was covered with abstract designs, or crosses, or series of dots, and in some cases by winged dragons, but at this time no sign of systematic heraldry can be seen.

Chapter Two

Chivalry

KNIGHTHOOD

0

The Anglo-Saxon word *cnicht*, from which comes our 'knight', means only 'household retainer' or 'servant'. This very clearly indicates the position of this class when they first appeared in England, although the knight of the later Middle Ages would probably not have liked to be reminded of his humble origin. During the first hundred years after Hastings, as the land settled down and large bodies of household knights became less necessary, many knights were provided by their lords with small estates, usually of a single manor, in place of wages. As lords of the manor, their duties being no longer purely military, they came within the feudal system, presiding in the court of their own manor and attending the honour- or estate-court of their overlord. Within a very short time of the Conquest these estates, known as knights' fees, had become hereditary, passing on the death of the original holder to the eldest son. Even a number of first-generation Norman knights are known to have married Englishwomen, and thus began the slow integration of the races.

As soon as the knight's fee became hereditary it was possible for it to pass to a woman or a child. Neither could be expected to serve in the Army in person, nor could an old or sick knight, so by about 1100 we find the payment of 'scutage', or 'shield money', paid by a knight annually in place of the actual service. The King was particularly glad to accept this money since it could be used to pay professional soldiers, who were more efficient than many rustic knights and able to serve for as long as was necessary in any theatre of war, whereas the knight only had to serve for forty days and was often unwilling to go overseas.

The knight of early Norman times was a professional soldier trained from childhood in the arts of war, horsemanship, wrestling, and the use of weapons – sword, lance, mace, axe, and bow – and of these the most important was the mastery of his steed. The horse must be taught to obey his master's commands precisely, to stand still in the turmoil of battle, to turn, move, and halt without the use of the rein, and to charge a wall of human beings or other horses. The French name for this horse-mastery – chivalry – became the name for the whole system of knighthood.

The knights themselves were generally brave and loyal but cruel, hard, and uncultured. It was the influence of the Church, the contact with the Saracens, and the holding of land that forged these coarse warriors into the bright sword of knighthood.

The Church taught forgiveness and gentleness and, by preaching the Crusades, used the knights' desire to fight in an attempt to regain the Holy Places from the Seljuk Turks. Many knights whose quarrels would have disturbed the peace at home joined the standard of the Holy War. Some of those who went were undoubtedly hoping to win estates in the conquered lands, others went in the hope of forgiveness for their sins, but many went swept up in a genuine wave of religious faith.

It was as a result of the First Crusade of 1095 that the early military orders were formed. These were fraternities of knights sworn to the monastic vow of poverty (the possessions of the order were held in common), chastity (marriage was forbidden), and obedience (to the rules of the order and of their superiors). They lived in communities apart, and their main task was the protection of pilgrims to the Holy Places and the defence of these places from the Infidel.

The first order was that of the Templars founded by a knight of Burgundy, named Hugh de Payens, with eight companions.

The Knights Templar

Their name derived from the position of their quarters near the Temple of Solomon in Jerusalem, and in 1128 St Bernard of Clairvaux drew up their rules for them. Their banner, half black and half white, 'they call Beauséant, because they are fair and friendly to the friends of Christ, to his enemies stern and black'. Inspired by the success of the Templars, the Master of the Hospital of St John in Jerusalem, Raymond of Le Puy, asked the Pope in 1130 for permission to convert it into a military order. The Knights of St John, or the Knights Hospitallers as they were called, together with the Templars, gathered recruits and wealth from those who could not serve themselves. They added to the growing sense of brotherhood and service of chivalry and, since they served together as a body, achieved a discipline and gained experience of warfare which they were able to pass on to the remainder of the knighthood. Chaucer's very perfect gentle knight had served in Prussia with another military order, the Teutonic Knights.

Those of the Crusaders who served for many years in Palestine came into contact with a luxurious and cultured way of life absolutely foreign to what they knew at home. They fought a foe as brave as themselves but one that could be magnanimous to a fallen enemy. No knight would wish to be less noble than Saladin, Sultan of Egypt and Syria, who once sent a gift of fruit to his sick foe, Richard of England, and on another occasion sent him a present of armour. Those of the Crusaders who returned to their homes took these new ideas back with them.

The third great force affecting the development of knighthood was the possession of land. This gave the knight a part in local government and, eventually, in Parliament, and brought wealth and the ability to live a more cultured life, to develop the arts of peace alongside the science of war.

By the twelfth century all these things began to separate those of

The Teutonic Knights

knightly class from the men-at-arms, the mercenary cavalry. Knighthood and chivalry became associated with gentle birth. The young man ending his period of military training was now received into the brotherhood of knighthood with fitting ceremony: the vigil in the Church, the ceremonial bath, the presentation of new robes, and the girding of the new knight with his sword and spurs, all became important parts of the ceremony, full of symbolism. Usually the young knight was struck a light blow with a sword or the hand on the shoulder or side of the neck, and some phrase, such as 'Be thou a good knight', was uttered.

At first, knighthood could be given by any knight. Latterly, it was usually given by a great baron or the King, and only occasionally by a knight if he was a captain of great renown.

Rising prices during the twelfth century had made weapons, horses, and armour more expensive and at the same time decreased the value of the sum charged for scutage. Many holders of knights' fees were therefore unwilling to take up knighthood, especially as their interest in the management of their manors and in local government increased. The growing usage of the payment of scutage made it simple to avoid serving. The first thirty-five years of the century had seen the strong government and internal peace of the reign of Henry I, and the service of the general levy of freemen had rarely been called for. The civil wars of Stephen's reign were largely fought with mercenaries, although the Battle of the Standard is a spectacular exception. After the chaos of this reign the general levy had largely lost its usefulness. By now it was also clear that the Conqueror had badly underestimated the number of knights the land could support. The time was ripe for drastic reorganisation.

Henry II, one of England's greatest administrators, set about the reorganisation. By the Inquest of 1166 he tried to record the precise number of his vassals, in order to obtain their services and taxes in full. By the Oath of 1169 he bound the knights and free tenants and all men over fifteen years old to himself personally. This was the logical conclusion of William the Conqueror's Oath of Salisbury and ensured that no one owed fealty to a baron only.

By the Assize of Arms in 1181 he reorganised the general levy. The basis of the levy was no longer to be land; it was to be wealth. Every freeman having goods worth ten marks was to serve in mail shirt, helmet, and with a spear. All other freemen were to have helmet, spear, and gambeson (a form of quilted armour discussed on page 45). In order to prevent the drain on the knighthood, all those holding knights' fees, whether they were actually knights or not, were to serve in mail shirt and helmet and with a shield and a spear.

An important development, at the end of this century, was the reduction in the number of knights required from each baron for continental campaigns in return for a much longer period of service. Richard I waged a series of campaigns in France for which an army of knights serving for only forty days would have been quite unsuitable. He hired mercenaries from Wales and Brabant, but for officers and heavy cavalry he needed knights, and these he got by asking his tenants-in-chief to serve for longer periods, each with only seven knights. Those knights who stayed at home seem to have paid the expenses of those who served. For short campaigns on the Scottish and Welsh Borders the full quota was still called for.

The shire and town levies were usually referred to as the 'Militia', and from now on they will be called by this name.

CRUSADER WARFARE

The major military undertaking of the twelfth century was the crusades: the attempt to win back the Holy Land from the infidels. Contact with a new enemy taught the Christians many fresh techniques, not least of them a new way of fighting.

The early medieval army, unless exceptionally large, was drawn up on the line of march in three groups called 'battles': the vanguard, the main guard, and the rear-guard. On reaching the field of battle, the same divisions were usually drawn up in a long line, sometimes with one division behind the other two as a reserve. Occasionally the three divisions were drawn up in lines one behind

39

the other. At Hastings the Norman Army was apparently in one long line with the archers and infantry in front of the cavalry. On the other hand, many continental armies consisted almost entirely of cavalry, and they sometimes attacked in waves, the following divisions attacking as soon as the one in front had spent its force.

On the Continent, infantry, with the exception of the mercenaries of Flanders, were not very highly considered by the knighthood. In England, however, the Saxon tradition of fighting on foot continued, and at battles like Tenchebrai in 1106 most of the knights were ordered to dismount and fight beside the infantry, while at the Battle of the Standard in 1138 we find the Norman knights fighting dismounted among the English militia under the banners of their local saints: St Peter of York, St John of Beverley, and St Wilfrid of Ripon. The older and more distinguished knights formed a guard around the standard of St Cuthbert on its cart at the centre of the army. The remainder of the knights formed the front rank, supported by the militia and the archers. All stood on the defensive as the English had at Hastings, but with much greater success against the unarmoured hordes of Galloway.

In Palestine the knighthood of Europe paid a terrible price for their reliance on heavy cavalry and their shortage of reliable infantry in the first years of the crusades. Swarms of well-horsed, lightly armed Turkish archers rode round the Christian army shooting down horse and man, melting away in front of the determined charges of the crusader cavalry, and closing in behind the retreating knights, until they fell helpless, exhausted by heat and lack of water. Dorylaeum, in 1097, was only prevented from becoming such a defeat by the sudden arrival, in the nick of time, of a second Christian force which fell on the rear of the Turks as they closed in for the kill.

The Christian knight could overthrow any Saracen horseman, less heavily armoured and less heavily mounted, who would face up to him. If the Saracen turned tail, however, he could rarely overtake him. The answer to the Turkish bowmen lay in the combination of cavalry, solid groups of infantry bowmen and spearmen, the choosing and holding of a position which could not be outflanked, and the adequate supply of the force on any long march so that horses and men were not weakened by starvation. The archers could fight the Saracens at long range, forcing them to close in and attack with sword and lance when the spearmen protected the archers. The Christian cavalry could then charge out from behind the infantry screen into the closely packed Saracens. If they were unsuccessful they could withdraw behind the infantry and prepare for another charge.

The first battle fought by this method was between the besieged Christians in Antioch and the besiegers under Kerboga, Emir of Mosul, in 1098. On this occasion the decision to rely heavily on the infantry may well have been taken because so many of the knights had lost their horses in the campaign. The Crusaders, marching out of the city and keeping the infantry on the side of the column towards the enemy, managed to place their line right across the plain so that the mountains at the edge prevented the Turks from outflanking them. A few thousand did get through before the gap was quite closed and by the damage they did showed how right the tactics of the Crusaders were. Had a larger force managed to break through the Christians would probably have been defeated and slaughtered.

The English played little part in the Holy Land until the Third Crusade. Richard I of England was a typical knight of Aquitaine, delighting in the glamour of the tournament, in the romantic poetry and songs of the troubadours, and in the love of beautiful women. He lacked the sense of responsibility to make a good king, and by his chivalric ideal of recapturing Jerusalem for the Faith he impoverished the Crown and neglected his kingdom. As a general, however, he was one of the finest produced by the Middle Ages. The Third Crusade was largely his own. His eighty-mile march along the coast of Palestine from Acre to Jaffa in the face of Saladin's army was brilliantly organised and carried out. First, to avoid the exhaustion and starvation that had beset so many previous expeditions, he arranged that his army should march only a few miles every day in the cool of the morning, that it should rest for a whole day every two or three days, and that it should march

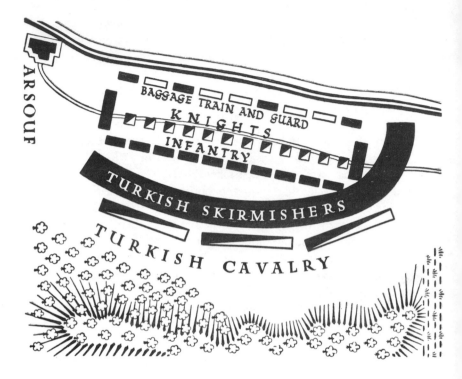

Plan of the Battle of Arsouf (1191)

along the coast where it could be supplied from the fleet which was to accompany it. By hugging the shore, he made certain that he could not be surrounded and that one flank of his army would always be free from attack.

Richard knew that he would be under continuous attack throughout the advance. His order of march must be his order of battle. He therefore drew up his cavalry in a long column of twelve squadrons with his Royal Standard on a cart in the middle. The ex-

42

perienced and highly trained cavalry of the Templars and Hospitallers led the van and brought up the rear. On the landward side a similar column of infantry kept the Turkish archers from shooting the horses of the knights, and the crossbowmen shot down the Saracens whenever they came too close. The remainder of the infantry marched along the other side of the cavalry column beside the sea and occasionally changed places with those on the enemy side.

Saladin's tactics were to keep the column under constant attack by part of his force, hoping to provoke the cavalry into breaking ranks, when it could be crushed by the remainder of his army, which he kept carefully hidden in the hills that border the narrow coastal plain. Such was Richard's command of his men, although of many races, and such was their confidence in him, that Saladin failed completely. He was finally driven to try an all-out attack at a point not far from the little town of Arsouf, where a forest which would hide his army until the last moment came down to within three miles of the sea.

The attacking Saracens fell in a vast horde upon the Crusaders, pressing most hard upon the rear-guard, perhaps in the hope that by delaying it a gap might be opened as the main body continued to advance. The Hospitallers, who were in the rear that day, suffered passively the loss of many of their horses under a hail of arrows. Eventually, they could stand it no longer and, turning on the foe, they charged out. Almost at the same moment Richard sounded the signal to attack, the call of six trumpets; the infantry opened gaps in their ranks and the cavalry poured out. The surprise was complete; the Saracens turned and fled. The four rear divisions of the Crusaders crashed into the tightly packed mass of their enemies, slaughtering and overturning them in thousands. The pursuit was short and controlled, for the Crusaders had lost too many fights by being cut down when scattered in pursuit of an apparently defeated foe. They rallied and returned to the army.

In the end, although Richard failed to take Jerusalem, he nevertheless undoubtedly prolonged the life of the Crusader Kingdom.

Chapter Three

The Twelfth Century

TWELFTH-CENTURY ARMOUR

Throughout the twelfth century the hauberk of mail continued to be the principal body defence of the wealthier troops. The Assize of Arms of 1181 requires it of the knights and all freemen with goods worth ten marks or more. The coif, or hood, was almost invariably made in one with the shirt, and in order that the head could get through the neckpiece this was made to open. When no enemy was expected the coif could hang on the shoulders. On the approach of the enemy it would be put on and the neck closed by drawing across it a flap, known as the 'ventail', which was then secured by a lace or strap and buckle on the side of the coif. The hauberk usually had long sleeves to the wrist, and, by the end of the century, the hands were enclosed by mail gloves attached to the end of the sleeves. These gloves consisted of two bags, one for the

Putting on the coif

Bishop Odo apparently wearing a scale hauberk (Bayeux Tapestry)

fingers and another for the thumb. The palm was covered in cloth or leather and was slit so that the hands could emerge when no fighting was taking place. A thong tied round the wrist prevented the sleeves from dragging with the weight of the mail.

Less wealthy troops, such as the townsmen and freemen of the 1181 Assize, wore only a gambeson. This was a tunic made of two thicknesses of cloth stuffed with wool, cotton, or old rags, and quilted like an eiderdown to keep the stuffing in position. Rather surprisingly, perhaps, this deadens a blow well and can be cut or pierced only with difficulty. Latterly, this quilted armour was worn under the hauberk as an additional defence, to take the weight of the mail and to prevent it rubbing the skin of the wearer. It was also called an 'aketon' from the Arabic name *al-qutun*, referring to its stuffing of cotton.

Some other forms of body-armour were already coming into use. Bishop Odo in the Bayeux Tapestry seems to be wearing a hauberk of overlapping scales, and these are common in the following century. They were made of iron or horn plates riveted to a cloth or leather garment; these plates overlapped like the scales of a fish. Gerald of Wales, writing in about 1200, describes some of the Norse attackers of Dublin in 1171 as wearing armour of iron plates, but whether of strips or of scales is not clear. William the Breton, writing in about 1225, but depicting a combat between the future Richard I and William des Barres, describes the lance piercing the shield, the hauberk, and the gambeson, and striking a plate of worked iron underneath all this.

Leg-armour was becoming more common, sometimes in the form of mail stockings, called 'hosen', tied up to the waist-belt under the hauberk, sometimes in the form of a mail strip which covered only the front of the leg and was laced around the back of it. Cloth hose were always worn under the mail since otherwise the rings would have cut into the flesh after a very short time.

Mail leg armour

45

Flat-topped helmets, one with a face-guard; about 1200

Conical helmets like those in the Bayeux Tapestry remained popular, usually with a nose-guard, often with a bar or flap guarding the back of the neck, sometimes with earflaps as well. Occasionally they were made deeper at the back to cover the nape. Towards the end of the century round-topped helmets appeared, and also cylindrical, flat-topped ones. Few men do not flinch instinctively from a blow struck at the face, and therefore many helmets of this period began to be fitted with a face-guard. This consisted of a semi-circular plate, curved to fit the face-opening of the coif, and attached to the lower edge of the helmet at the front. It was pierced with horizontal slits for the eyes and with many small holes over the area of the mouth to let in the air. The helmet was held on by

Helmet with ear-flaps; about 1200

Helmet extended to guard the neck; 1128

laces tied under the chin to prevent it from being knocked off in battle or, worse, knocked sideways so that the wearer was temporarily blinded. This happened to Guy de Montfort at the battle of Tagliacozzo, and, blindly lashing out, he accidentally wounded his friend Alard de St Valéry who was going to his rescue.

The little twelfth-century ivory chessmen found in a sand-dune in Lewis, in the Hebrides, include a number wearing a new form of helmet, the 'kettle-hat', so-called because of its resemblance to a cauldron, at that time called a kettle. Two kinds are shown on the chessmen: one is round-topped with a narrow brim, the other conical with a deep and steep-sided conical brim. They were worn with or without the coif and were laced or strapped under the

Kettle hat worn by one of the Lewis chessmen; about 1200

British Army helmet; 1915

chin. Throughout the period when armour was worn, this type of helmet remained popular with the infantry and with those knights who found the all-enclosing helm too confining. It was particularly useful for siege work, since missiles discharged from a wall top travel downwards, and a brim can deflect them from the face as easily as a face-guard and does not restrict the view. This type of helmet was revived as a shrapnel helmet for the British Army in 1915.

The large kite-shaped shield continued in use for a while but was given a straight top edge, presumably to make it easier to see over. Anna Comnena, the daughter of the Emperor of Byzantium, wrote a description of the Crusaders on their way to the Holy Land, in which she says that their shields were metal-covered and highly polished. By the end of the twelfth century a rather smaller shield of similar shape was in use by horsemen. Some types of infantry continued to carry large shields until the end of the fifteenth century.

When the lance was couched beneath the arm during the charge the shield was now allowed to hang in front of the rider from a neckstrap. It was only after the lance had been broken or dropped that the horseman, drawing his sword, passed his left arm through the loops on the back of the shield and grasped the handgrip so as to be able to manœuvre it to parry blows.

By about 1150 a number of knights were painting on their shields devices which, at a later date, appeared again on the shields of their sons. The tomb of Geoffrey, Count of Anjou, ancestor of the Plantagenet kings of England, bears a shield covered in golden lions, the ancestor of the lions of England. This was the beginning of heraldry, a system of identification which was enormously elaborated during the Middle Ages. At first the devices were animals or birds or simple geometric shapes chosen to decorate the shield of the knight, either to identify himself to his companions and

Geoffrey, Count of Anjou, from his tomb

47

followers in the turmoil of battle or in order to distinguish him in the tournament. When his son succeeded to his estates the former would also adopt the device on his father's shield. Later, a system of small differences was devised to distinguish younger sons and branches of great families. They, and even unrelated but dependent families, would adopt variations of the main device with additions or in different colours.

Heraldic differences

In the second half of this century knights began to wear a loose flowing linen garment over their hauberks. It was shaped like a tube, caught on the shoulders, belted at the waist and slit almost half-way up at front and back so that it fell easily on either side of the saddle. Occasionally it had short, or even cuff-length, sleeves. These 'gowns' as they were called, were at first invariably made of white or self-coloured cloth, and it was not until the following century that the device on the knight's shield was also used to decorate his gown. The purpose of the garment is not known. A contemporary writer described it as protecting the hauberk from the rain but as the head, neck, arms, legs, and, when in the saddle, the skirts were all open to the rain its protective value must have been slight. It might have given some protection from the heat of the sun in the Holy Land. On the other hand, it may simply have been copied from the Saracens or from the Byzantines, both of whom wore similar garments.

The gown worn over armour

48

TWELFTH-CENTURY ARMS

The sword remained the chief weapon of both cavalry and infantry. The blade was usually longer than formerly and more pointed, so that the weapon could be used for thrusting. The fuller was usually much narrower than before. The guard above the hand was usually straight but occasionally the ends curved up towards the blade. Tea-cosy- and Brazil-nut-shaped pommels remained popular, but a new type of pommel also came into use. This was disc-shaped and, from about 1180, often had a strongly bevelled edge or a raised centre. Although these swords sometimes look heavy and rather clumsy, the large pommel counterbalances the weight of the blades and they are easily wielded.

A sword of the 12th century

The battle-axe on a three- or four-foot-long shaft was very popular as a secondary weapon among the Anglo-Norman knights, both on foot and on horse. The Normans probably learnt its value from the Saxons during the Conquest and the subsequent revolts, Saxon and baronial.

The lance remained unchanged, but from the beginning of the twelfth century a stout ring was sometimes fitted over the shaft immediately behind the hand. It was thrust against the armpit by the force of a blow and prevented the lance from being pushed back under the arm.

Many of the peasantry, and others who would not normally

Sword with disc-shaped pommel

Axe of the 12th century

possess weapons, answered the call of Peter the Hermit and went on the First Crusade. They took with them whatever weapons lay to hand: the huntsman his boar-spear, the woodman and carpenter their axes. The peasants attached their sickles and hedging bills to staves, or took up a hayfork, a flail, or a large fencing mallet; others carried a club fitted with iron spikes. From these simple arms whole families of weapons were developed and became the typical infantry weapons of later periods.

It was during the conquest of Ireland (1169–75) that we first hear of the Norman barons of the Welsh borders using the lightly armed Welsh archers of Gwent and Morganwg with their bows 'neither made of horn, ash, nor yew, but of elm: ugly unfinished-looking weapons but astonishingly stiff, large and strong, and equally capable of use for long or short shooting'. Gerald of Wales describes the Welsh archers at the siege of Abergavenny Castle in 1182, sending their arrows through an oak door four inches thick so that the steel heads showed through on the other side. One knight, it is said, was pinned to his horse by an arrow through hauberk, hosen, leg, and saddle. It was this bow that was to become the English longbow and the principal agent of the English victories of the Hundred Years War. At this time it was only used by the Welsh, and the numerous missile-carrying infantry in the armies of both Richard I and John were mercenary crossbowmen. Mounted crossbowmen were also used, while light cavalry armed with the simple bow were particularly popular in the Crusader Kingdom of the Holy Land in imitation of the Turkish mounted archers.

Early infantry weapons

 TWELFTH-CENTURY CASTLES

Two great stone towers were built almost immediately after the Conquest, the keeps of the Tower of London and of Colchester

50

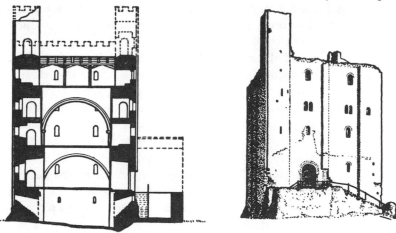

A Norman tower; Hedingham, about 1135

Castle, but in the following century this type of tower became more common. In general, they are massive buildings, usually square in plan, with shallow buttresses clasping the corners and running up the centre of each face. Early examples are usually two stories high. The lower story consists of cellars and storerooms and usually contains a well; there is no external doorway and access is by a staircase from the first floor. The first floor is divided into two rooms of unequal size, the larger being the great hall, the main living accommodation of the castle. The entrance is usually through this room, and is reached by an external stairway which rises along one face of the tower and was often enclosed in a defensive fore-building. In early towers the 'solar', the living and sleeping quarters of the owner or his constable, is in the smaller division of this floor which also often contains a small chapel. In later towers the solar and chapel are usually raised on the second floor over the hall. Above this was a steep wooden roof hidden by the surrounding walls which had a walk all the way round for the defenders. The upper levels could be reached from the hall by spiral staircases in the thickness of the wall at the corners of the building. Some towers had small turrets at roof level on the top of these stairs. The thick walls usually contain small rooms and the latrines.

The defence of these types of tower was largely passive, and they were only used when the outer bailey was in enemy hands. The garrison then shut themselves up in the tower and hurled missiles down upon the heads of the attackers from the wall-walks. The walls, anything up to fifteen foot thick near the base, would take weeks to burrow through, by which time relief might have come or the attackers have run out of supplies.

A less expensive method of converting a motte-and-bailey castle to a stone one was to replace the palisades on the mound and rampart by stone walls and retain the wooden buildings within, as, for instance, was done at Windsor.

The motte-and-bailey castle was particularly vulnerable to fire, and the Bayeux Tapestry actually shows the Normans setting fire to Dinan while Duke Conan of Brittany hastily surrenders the keys to Duke William. The multiplication of stone castles in the twelfth century was undoubtedly due partly to this danger and partly to the improved siege techniques brought back by the Crusaders.

In no phase of medieval life was the debt to the Romans greater than in siegecraft. The medieval siege was carried out in much the same way as the Roman one, and several siege-engines described by Roman writers were used in the Middle Ages. The simplest of these was the ballista, which was no more than a gigantic crossbow hurling huge arrows and occasionally stones. This could be used with considerable accuracy even as an anti-personnel weapon. The second engine was the 'mangonel', or catapult, which the Romans had called the 'onager', or wild ass. It consisted of a heavy wooden trestle mounted on a strong horizontal frame. At the foot of the trestle was a thick skein of sinews or cords (Roman writers advised the use of women's hair) through the middle of which ran a stout beam. The skein was tightly twisted by means of a capstan at each end, thus forcing the beam vertically and very tightly against the crossbar of the trestle; the capstans were then

Mangonel about to be released

locked into position. At this point a windlass was used to haul the beam back to the horizontal, thus further increasing the tension on the skein. The missile, a ball of stone or lead, was next placed in a cup at the end of the beam. When the beam was released the tension on the skein snapped the beam back to the vertical position where it struck the crossbar, catapulting the missile off with considerable velocity. This was a bombardment weapon suitable for breaking down palisades and stone walls.

The normal method of attacking a castle or walled town can be briefly described as follows: after the garrison had been summoned to surrender and had refused, the walls could be assaulted by scaling parties with tall ladders. Covering fire would be given by archers and crossbowmen, who usually stood behind large

Archer shooting from behind a pavise

53

shields, called 'pavises', to protect them from the missiles of the garrison. They would try to clear the garrison off the wall-walk to give the scaling parties time to climb up. The garrison would try to push the ladders down and, by hurling stones and other missiles, prevent the attackers reaching the wall top. If this attack failed, a real siege was resorted to. The town or castle would be surrounded so that casualties and hunger would weaken the defence, since help and supplies could not then be sent in. Siege-engines would be built, and a bombardment opened. If the walls were very strong, or a great tower was involved, against which the mangonels would be ineffective, a mine was dug under one corner. This was a tunnel, the roof of which was supported by timbers. The cavity under the corner of the tower would be made as large as possible, and when all was ready the mine would be filled with combustible material and set on fire, so that as soon as the wood supports were burnt away the whole corner would come crashing down and an assault could be sent in over the ruins. If the castle was built on a rock or there was a water-filled ditch, mining was impossible, and then a battering-ram or giant screw was used to break into the masonry at the foot of the wall. The ditch would have to be filled up first, then the ram or screw brought forward under cover of a stoutly built, movable shed. This would be covered with fresh cowhides to prevent the garrison setting fire to it with fire-arrows. The ram, which was a huge tree trunk with an

Battering ram in action

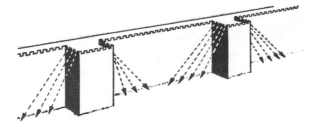

The foot of the walls covered from the tops of
the wall towers

iron-shod point, was hung by ropes from the roof of the shed and
swung backwards and forwards by its team so that the point
smashed again and again into the masonry, slowly picking out a
hole. The screw was similarly used to bore a hole. The defenders
could lower mattresses over the wall to deaden the blow, or hooks
to catch the head of the ram or screw. Sometimes the shed contained only men equipped with picks and crowbars to dig their
way through the masonry. The Norse attackers at Rothesay
Castle hewed their way through the soft sandstone wall with their
axes. The surest defence was to smash the shed or its occupants
with great stones dropped from the walls, as 'Black Agnes', wife
of the Earl of Dunbar, did in her defence of Dunbar Castle, in
1339.

   If all else failed, the besiegers could build great wheeled towers
called 'belfries' and push them up to the walls. Archers stationed
in the top could then clear the wall-walks, and a drawbridge could
be dropped on to the wall allowing the assault troops to cross. They
were however extremely expensive to make, difficult to manœuvre,
very vulnerable to shots from the garrison's mangonels, and were
sometimes successfully set alight.

   The Crusaders were deeply impressed by the countermeasures
to these methods adopted by the Byzantines and Saracens. The
best defence against attackers at the wall-foot is flanking fire along

Siege-tower

Trebuchet; hauling down the arm. 1. ready to shoot; 2. shooting

the wall, and both the Byzantines and Saracens had achieved this by placing along the walls projecting towers, from the top of which the base of the main wall could be covered. The enormous height of the walls of towns such as Acre and Antioch made attack by ladders very difficult. Towards the end of the twelfth century a new engine came into use, the 'trebuchet', which, unlike the mangonel, was a high trajectory sling hurling huge stones of two or three hundredweight high in the air. The only defence against it was higher walls, and these are particular vulnerable to undermining, so the provision of flanking towers became even more essential.

The castles built by Henry II and his subjects are therefore very different from those of their predecessors. In order to avoid the danger of a mine under the corner of the keep, Henry built towers like Orford in Suffolk (1165–73), which is polygonal with three

56

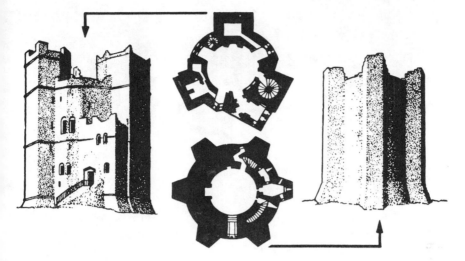

Left, Orford (1165–1173)
Right, Conisborough; about 1170

flanking towers which command the bases of the walls. Others of his contemporaries built completely round keeps, like that at Pembroke built by one of the Earls Marshal in about 1200. At the same time, what are called 'curtain-wall castles' became popular. These had a high surrounding wall to protect them against trebuchet shots, with projecting towers at intervals so that the whole base of the wall could be commanded by archers on the towers. At first these towers were made square, but later, in order to avoid the danger of mining, the part projecting outwards was made round and thus without corners. The towers broke up the wall walk, so that any attacker reaching the walk would have to fight his way into a tower in order to reach the next stretch of walk or a stair down into the town or castle. The high walls made the great keep unnecessary, and new castles in England were usually built without one; instead, the tower in which the constable or owner lived was made rather bigger than the others. Dover (about 1180)

57

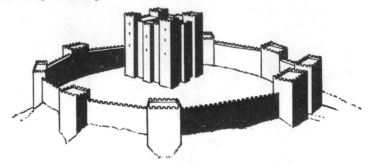

A twelfth-century 'curtain-wall castle'

and Framlingham in Suffolk (about 1200) are examples of curtain-wall castles. The high walls of Dover defied the trebuchets of Louis the Dauphin in 1217 when the older type of castle was forced to surrender.

Chapter Four

The Thirteenth Century

THIRTEENTH-CENTURY ORGANISATION

Henry III (1216–72) inherited a curtailed feudal force, a reorganised militia, and a considerable number of mercenaries. The paid household troops were particularly important. Consisting of about one hundred knights, a similar number of mounted sergeants, and a rather larger body of infantry and archers, they formed the nucleus of the feudal army and served as its officers. On the other hand, John's incompetence and the eagerness of the barons to increase their own privileges had weakened the Royal authority. The newly reduced quotas of men became customary, and, instead of serving for longer as they had originally agreed, the barons insisted on the old forty days' limit. The efficiency of the army was further lowered by an increasing shortage of knights. They were now set apart by rank from the other mounted men-at-arms and were valued at twice their worth, but the growing expense of the ceremony of knighthood and the knight's rapidly increasing judicial duties made many people unwilling to be knighted.

King Henry III overcame this shortage of knights, a vital branch of the army, by issuing orders, usually just before a campaign, that all those holding a knight's fee or having an income of £20 a year should be knighted. The goods of those who failed to do so were to be seized by the sheriff. This was not just a method of raising money, since the fine was returned to anyone who actually served. By the end of the reign, in 1272, four-fifths of those liable had become knights.

Henry continued to use and improve the militia all through his reign. Royal officials, called Commissioners of Array, inspected the freemen of the county, swearing them to arms and choosing those most suitable for the King's service. The King might require axemen or horsemen or archers, depending on where he was campaigning. The best armed four, six, or eight men would be chosen from each vill, and forty days' provisions would be given them at the expense of 'the community', which probably means those lucky enough not to be chosen. Even as early as this there were confidence tricksters who accepted money from each of the chosen men to serve in his place and then ran off with it. The villeins were now sworn to arms as well as the freemen. For the first time the militia were paid for services outside their own county.

Henry III's set of military orders, called the Assize of Arms of 1242, was of great importance. It was originally a police measure, dealing with the keeping of the peace, but it divided the classes into the main branches of the army which lasted throughout the Middle Ages. For the first time the more well-to-do, those with an income of £15 a year, were to serve on horseback. This produced the light cavalry necessary to augment the knights and was probably introduced because many people were ceasing to serve as cavalry since horses were now more expensive. The second most important part of this Assize ordered all those with incomes of between £2 and £5 to have bows. Although these were almost certainly not yet longbows it was the members of this class that were to become the famous archers of the next century. These were the foundations of the two groups that were to beat the French in the Hundred Years War.

This Assize was reissued in 1285, with little change, as the Statute of Winchester and remained in force until 1558. It is important because, whenever later kings were accused of demanding too much service from the militia, their subjects appealed to this Statute.

Edward I, with his great territorial ambitions, required an efficient army and one that could serve for long periods. His reputation as a leader in the civil wars of his father's reign and on his Crusade, and his love of chivalry, made him very popular with his baronage, who were willing to co-operate with him. A trade boom and the development of the department of the Royal Household called the Wardrobe as a financial department gave the King the wealth and organisation to build an efficient army. Unfortunately, in order to achieve this efficiency he both gave up many Royal rights and ended his reign bankrupt.

Payment to the troops was normally made in Edward I's reign (1272–1307) and was necessary because more men were required to serve outside the borders of the realm.

Barons still brought their reduced quotas of men but often served themselves as paid captains.

The militia were paid by the King, either from the moment of leaving their county or at least from the place of mustering with other groups; up to that moment they were paid from county funds.

Edward I began the practice of giving individual captains contracts to provide bodies of mercenaries to serve indefinitely.

Since Edward's tactics required cavalry and archers, he encouraged knighthood both by chivalric display and by heavy fines on those who failed to be knighted. At the end of the reign those with an income of £40 a year had to be knighted and this remained the level for most of the Middle Ages. The main part of Edward's infantry usually consisted of archers, and the orders sent to the sheriffs to recruit men most often called for this class, together with the cavalry. The regular and successful co-operation of these two classes, the archers (the £2 freeholders), and the knighthood together with the £15 freeholders, both in the field and the law courts, undoubtedly founded the well-knit armies of the Hundred Years War. Whereas the French chivalry despised their infantry, the English cavalry respected theirs. The well-trained and experienced infantry of the Welsh Marches were particularly popular for the Scottish campaigns.

Edward probably organised the administration and command of his army in the field in groups of 20, 100, and 1,000 men (pay-

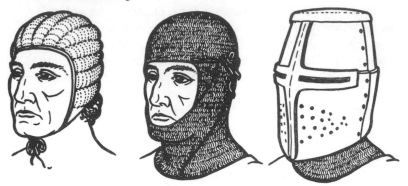

Arming cap, coif with ventail, and helm, all about 1250

lists include officers called vintenaries, centenaries, and millenaries), although the exact details of this structure are uncertain.

THIRTEENTH-CENTURY ARMOUR

At the beginning of the century, the knight's armour consisted of a mail hauberk with a built-in coif and long sleeves, together with mail hosen. This remained the commonest form of armour for the cavalry throughout the century. Under the coif was worn a tight-fitting quilted cap to give additional protection to the head. The helm, at first invariably flat-topped, became deeper at the back until it was more or less cylindrical but sometimes curved in under the chin to protect the throat. The slits for the eyes ('sights') were strengthened all round by bars of steel, and a vertical strip strengthened the front of the helm. Since the slits were close to the eyes it was quite easy to see out. The lower part of the front was pierced by many small holes to let in air.

Many knights preferred to wear the coif alone, or with a kettle-hat instead of a helm. By about 1250 the coif was sometimes made separately from the hauberk, and illustrations show that it was

Nasal helmet of the 13th century

sometimes lined. One Saracen writer mentions mail lined with rabbits' fur. The nasal helmet continued to be worn and was sometimes round-topped. Towards the end of the century the nose-guard disappeared, and the round-topped helmet was occasionally worn under the coif.

Mail protects against sword cuts but a heavy blow from a mace or axe might break bones inside, even without cutting the mail, or a strong thrust from a pointed weapon might force the rings apart. In order to give extra protection to the neck, a form of stiff, upright collar, laced at the front, which may have had steel plates inside, was worn over the mail. As an alternative to the mail hauberk, one of iron scales was often worn. By the end of the century the mail gauntlets were sometimes made with separate fingers, and we read of gauntlets of steel or whalebone in use on the Continent. Small saucer-shaped plates were occasionally fixed to the elbows and, by the end of the century, to the shoulders also.

The legs of a cavalryman are particularly vulnerable to the infantry, and so attention was paid to their defence. From about 1220 horsemen wore quilted tubes over their thighs, and a little later solid knee-caps were attached to the mail or strapped over it. Towards the end of the century these two defences were combined, and the knee-caps were attached to the thigh defences. Very occasionally, gutter-shaped plates were worn to protect the shins but these were never common until the fourteenth century. The horseman gained extra protection from the high back of the saddle which curved around his hips, and the saddle-bow which shielded the stomach.

Solid body-armour was apparently in use on the Continent early in the thirteenth century and in England by the second half of this century. On two tomb effigies, in the opening of the gown beneath the arm can be seen what is apparently a breast and backplate, joined together by straps down the side. One English manuscript

Knee-caps attached to quilted thigh defences

63

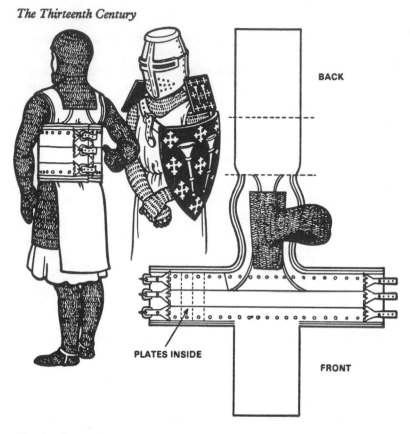

BACK

PLATES INSIDE

FRONT

Poncho-like body-armour. The knight on the right wears ailettes

shows similar waist-length garments apparently reinforced by plates. This is probably the *cuirie* of contemporary documents. The name suggests that they were made of leather, from the French *cuir*. Some knights who served abroad no doubt brought back Continental body-armours; these were either gowns lined with plates, or poncho-like garments, the upper part of which contained plates, with broad flaps, also steel-lined, passing under the arms and buckling at the back.

Body-armour opening down the side

64

Body-armour; probably a 'cuirie'

It was difficult to recognise a knight in action when his face was covered by his helm. In some cases the wearer's device was painted on the side of his helm or on a fan of parchment and copper or light wood placed on top of the helm. By the end of this century true 'crests', usually decorative animals, made in the round, were used, possibly mainly for the tournament rather than for war. Probably so that the knight could be recognised from the side, his heraldic arms (i.e. coat-of-arms) were painted on flat rectangles, diamonds, or discs, called 'ailettes', attached to the points of the shoulder. Piers Gaveston, the notorious favourite of Edward II, had a pair made of parchment decorated with pearls.

Barons and knights with large retinues had a flag, known as a 'banner', carried on a lance before them. It was rectangular, with the longest side attached to the shaft. The arms of the owner were embroidered or painted on the surface, which was probably stiffened to make it stand out so that it was clearly visible as a rallying point for the retinue. The ordinary knight usually carried a triangular pennant, sometimes with the shortest side, sometimes with the longer side against the lance.

Knightly shield

The knightly shield was now usually smaller and shaped like the bottom of an electric iron and was sometimes slightly curved round the user's body to give greater protection.

By the middle of the century horses sometimes had mail coverings. These were usually made in two parts divided at the saddle; the fore part reached down to the knee and covered the head except for the nose, mouth, and eyes; the rear part reached down to the hocks. This type of armour must always have been rare because of its weight and cost. Most of the horse armours used in Edward's campaigns were probably of leather or quilting. By the end of the century leather horse helmets, called 'chanfrons', were in use.

The better-armed infantry wore either the full hauberk with coif, or a shorter form with elbow-length sleeves and no coif, prob-

Knightly pennants

65

Heavy cavalry and infantry of the 13th century

ably called the 'haubergeon'. Apparently they did not usually wear leg-armour; the difficulty of marching in mail hose as well as the cost of buying them would have discouraged their use. The infantry usually wore kettle-hats, skull-caps, or sometimes no headpiece at all. The gambeson of the 1181 Assize of Arms must have been quite common, but many of the infantry, and especially the archers, had no armour except helmets. When fighting on foot all ranks sometimes used a small round shield, called a 'buckler', held by a central handle at the back. This was used at arm's length for parrying blows, particularly when fighting with swords.

In the thirteenth century there were already professional fencing-masters teaching the art of swordsmanship; but a Statute of the City of London of 1286 forbids the keeping of fencing schools or the teaching of the art within the City.

Sword and buckler

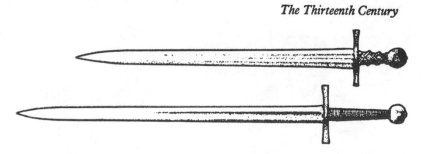

Two thirteenth-century swords; the longer one is a 'sword of war'

THIRTEENTH-CENTURY ARMS

The sword remained the main knightly weapon of this period. It was not only used by those of gentle birth but was carried by anyone who could afford one or had picked one up after a battle.

The cross-guards were usually longer than formerly and either straight or turned up slightly towards the blade. Occasionally, the extreme ends of the guards were turned up sharply. Pommels were usually of the wheel-shape already described but were quite often trefoils, quatrefoils, or simple spheres. Blades were longer than before but still had a wide fuller running the full length. The introduction of solid body-armour towards the end of the century probably accounts for the development of some longer and heavier swords with thirty-eight-inch blades and hilts which could be wielded with both hands when necessary. These are called 'swords of war' in contemporary descriptions and inventories.

Special swords designed principally for thrusting came into use late in the century. Their blades are sharply pointed and made stiffer than before with diamond-shaped cross-section. They could pierce the rings of mail, bursting them apart, or could be thrust between the joints of plate armour.

The scabbard hung on the left hip from a broad leather belt. The buckle end of the belt was attached to the top of the sheath, and the other end, which passed round the back of the wearer, a few inches lower. This caused the sheath to hang at a slight angle and helped to prevent it getting between the wearer's legs and tripping

Left, a knight of the Trumpington family about 1300. *Right*, the fastenings of the sword-belt

him up. On formal occasions and in civil life the sword, sheathed and with its belt wrapped round it, was carried by a squire or, in the case of a king or emperor, by his marshal or constable.

Short stabbing daggers, usually rather like miniature swords, began to be worn even by the knightly classes. They were usually carried in the belt on the right side. They were held in the hand, point downwards, and were only used as a last resort when other weapons were broken or lost, or at very close quarters.

'Falchions', single-edged swords with very wide blades often with a curved cutting edge and with the widest part of the blade near the point, were also popular in the thirteenth and fourteenth

Thirteenth-century dagger

68

centuries. The distribution of the weight far up the blade would give them great shearing force. Most falchions had hilts like normal swords but a few were fitted to a short wooden shaft by means of a socket.

Various other experimental sword-like weapons were being tried out, including single-edged blades attached to handles curved like an umbrella handle, probably to give some protection to the knuckles.

Falchion; about 1270 (Durham Cathedral)

The Danish-axe remained very popular, especially for fighting on foot; some were fitted on shafts about six foot long. The mighty blows given with such an axe put a great strain on the shaft immediately below the head and to lessen this the socket was often extended down the shaft for three or four inches. Probably for the same reason the lower point of the very largest axes was occasionally extended downwards and twisted round the shaft to form a second socket.

Smaller axes, shaped like tomahawks, were also used, particularly on horseback. These had a long sharp spike on the back of the blade as an alternative weapon.

A great variety of clubs and maces was popular. These range from heavy wooden truncheons covered all over with iron studs to short wooden shafts with metal heads with steel flanges or pyramidal knobs.

Thirteenth-century mace

69

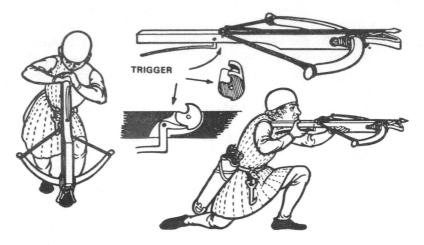

Spanning and shooting a crossbow

The spear for both cavalry and infantry remained unchanged. Hayforks, flails, and hedging bills were used by the infantry.

The longbow is not specifically mentioned by name in the various Assizes of Arms but no doubt the English archers appreciated its obvious advantages over the native English bow. In the Welsh wars of Edward I they would be at the receiving end of it, and during the Scottish campaigns they served alongside Edward's very large numbers of Welsh infantry. English archers usually carried their arrows in a bundle tucked, point upwards, through a loop on their belts. Mounted archers normally carried them in a quiver attached to their belts or hung on the saddle.

The crossbow was now being made with a heavier bow and was fitted with a stirrup in front of the stock. The crossbowman had a metal hook hung from the centre of his waist-belt. To span the bow the man, kneeling on one knee, put his other foot into the stirrup, fixed the hook under the string, and then straightened up until the string was pulled up over a catch on the stock. (Since crossbow arrows usually had heads of square cross-section they were called

Sling in use; staff-slings with bottle and stone

'quarrels' from the French word *carré*.) Crossbowmen usually carried their quarrels in a quiver on the waist-belt. The bow was often made of long strips of horn stuck together like plywood and covered with parchment, forming a particularly powerful and springy bow.

The sling, one of the simplest and earliest of missile weapons, was still in use. It consisted of a shallow pocket for the stone, with two cords at opposite ends. Both cords were held in the right hand and the stone placed in the pocket. The sling was then whirled round. When full speed was reached one cord was released just before the stone reached the top of its circuit, so that it flew out of the pocket in a high arc. Slings were also used to throw lead bullets. A trained man could achieve considerable accuracy, as the story of David and Goliath shows. An improved version, the staff-sling, had one cord attached to a short stick to give greater range – a sort of hand trebuchet. Paintings sometimes show these throwing bottles which may have been full of some inflammable material or of quicklime. The latter formed a cloud of choking and blinding dust rather like poisonous gas in its effect. Apparently in naval war soft-soap was also used, so that the enemy would slip about on their own decks.

THIRTEENTH-CENTURY TACTICS

In the battles of the Barons' War of the middle of the thirteenth century the bulk of the fighting seems to have been done by the cavalry, the infantry being in support, as at Lewes in 1264. Infantry casualties on the losing side were heavy since they were unable to escape from the field in the way that the cavalry were.

The campaign of Evesham (1265) is important because it shows the future Edward 1 as a general with a grasp of strategy unusual in the Middle Ages. At the beginning of the year the King and Prince Edward were prisoners in the hands of Earl Simon de Montfort and the Baronial party. The Baronial forces were

71

divided. Earl Simon and his Welsh allies were mopping up pockets of Royalist resistance on the west side of the River Severn; the forces of his son, the younger Simon, were besieging Pevensey Castle, a Royalist stronghold in Sussex. Prince Edward escaped and gathered together an army of loyal barons and those who had deserted the Baronial cause. Edward now showed the quality of his generalship, that was later to conquer Wales. He held the line of the Severn and successfully prevented de Montfort from crossing back into England, destroying bridges and fords, capturing Gloucester which the rebels had garrisoned as a crossing point, and destroying a fleet prepared at Bristol to ferry the Earl across. Meanwhile, the younger Simon moved slowly to his father's aid by a roundabout route, presumably gathering in all his allies on the way. He eventually arrived at Kenilworth. Prince Edward, at Worcester, was exactly between the two Baronial armies. To avoid being caught in a pincer movement and to prevent his opponents from combining, the Prince had to act at once. Abandoning his watch on the River Severn, he marched swiftly to Kenilworth and annihilated the Baronial army by a dawn attack which caught them still in their beds. He returned at once to guard the river crossings, but too late, since Earl Simon had already crossed at Kempsey, downstream from Worcester, and was marching towards Kenilworth via Evesham, unaware of his son's defeat. The Prince, hearing of his enemies' movements, divided his army into three corps, with orders to converge on Evesham. The Earl was caught with his own small force, at the bottom of a slope within the loop of a river, with two Royal armies closing the open side of the loop and the third force on the far bank cutting off all retreat. The result, in spite of the personal courage of the Earl, was a foregone conclusion.

The Welsh wars of Edward I saw the gradual perfection of the new organisation and the new tactics. By 1298 Edward, with an army consisting of heavy cavalry acting in unison with archers, defeated the Guardian of Scotland, William Wallace, at Falkirk. The English army was paid by the King and the value of each man's horse had been recorded, so that if it were killed the King could repay the owner the true price. On this occasion, the greater part of the archers were probably still Welshmen or troops from the Welsh Marches.

The Scots, who intended to fight a defensive battle, were drawn up on a hillside in four great circles of spearmen, supported by some archers and a small group of cavalry which Wallace kept in reserve. The front of the army was defended by a marsh, impassable for cavalry.

Edward drew up his army in three divisions. He opened the battle with flank attacks by cavalry, a frontal attack across the marsh having been found impossible. The English were flung back by the dense ranks of Scottish spearmen who stood 'impenetrable as a wood', but not before the Scots archers had been killed or scattered. The leaders of the Scots cavalry led their men off without striking a blow: they were very greatly outnumbered and were also probably jealous of Wallace, a gentleman but not one of the nobility.

The Scots foot were now at the mercy of Edward's archers, their own bowmen dead or scattered and without their cavalry who might have dispersed the English archers. Unable to advance under the threat of cavalry attack, they fell where they stood until the English cavalry could ride into the circles through the broken ranks.

THIRTEENTH-CENTURY CASTLES

The relatively peaceful reign of Henry III saw few new castles being built in England. It was a period of improving the living accommodation, of rebuilding and beautifying within the walls, of building larger chapels and fine halls for banquets and courts, and even of laying out flower gardens and orchards. The typical castle of the reign, such as Barnwell in Northamptonshire, built in 1264, is square with a tower at each corner. Because of the danger from mining, a low site was chosen so that the walls could be surrounded by a water-filled moat. The gateway of such castles was either under a large wall tower or between two closely placed wall towers.

The reigns of Edward I, his son, and, most of all, his grandson,

73

were periods of peace at home and war abroad. ('Abroad' then still included Wales, Scotland, and Ireland.) The need for new castles in England was slight, and the square plan with corner towers and a moat remained the usual form for small residential castles as long as these were built. In the troublesome times of the fifteenth century they could not stand up to a prolonged siege but were quite capable of keeping out an enraged neighbour until his anger or purse was spent. The later ones have more comfortable and convenient buildings within their walls and, in the centre of one wall, a gatehouse with towers, copying those of the great Royal castles of Edward I's reign.

The next period of English castle-building began with Edward I's conquest of Wales and his attack on Scotland. The Welsh were subdued not so much by battles as by surrounding the Principality with the great Royal fortresses from which the natives could be overawed. The castle of Flint, built at the end of Edward's first Welsh campaign of 1276–7, is still of the earlier type, four-square with corner towers, one of which was still made larger to act as a keep and was built outside the bailey in the old fashion.

However, Edward had been a Crusader and had seen the highly developed castles of the Holy Land. There, the defence of the castle was not by a single curtain wall but by two or more walls, so that if the outer defences fell the garrison could retire into the inner defences, which would be high enough to overlook the wall-walk of the outer wall. At Krak-des-Chevaliers in Syria, built in about 1205 by the Knights Hospitallers, a massive curtain wall with huge towers is completely surrounded by an outer wall with many wall towers partly separated from the inner work by a water-filled ditch. The greatest of the Edwardian castles of Wales follow this plan, and combine with it elaborate defences for the gateway – always the most vulnerable point. Beaumaris Castle in Anglesey, begun in 1295 as a result of the final Welsh revolt, is a great square of towering walls with massive round towers at each corner and towers of D-shaped plan on two sides. In the centre of each of the other two sides is one of the new gatehouses. These can best be described as a combination of the square tower with the gateway

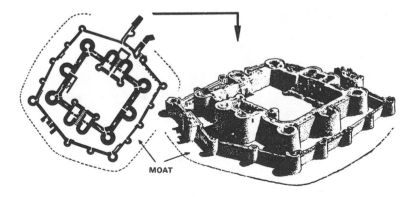

Krak-des-Chevaliers; about 1205

passing under it and the type flanked by two wall towers. The new gatehouse has two great drum towers bulging towards the field, between which is a pit covered by a drawbridge; behind these towers and built on to them is a square block under which the roadway passes. Even if the enemy broke through the drawbridge and

MOAT

Beaumaris Castle, 1295

75

the outer portcullis, they had to fight their way up this long passage to the doors at the inner end past other portcullises. If the lower part of the gatehouse fell into enemy hands, there was no internal staircase to reach the upper stories.

The inner castle of Beaumaris is surrounded by a low outer wall with many small towers, outside which is a moat. The outer gates are not built opposite the inner ones, so that if an enemy captured them he would have to attack along the front of the main wall to reach the main gates. Most of these castles have a number of gates so that the garrison could sally out on horseback to make counterattacks on the back of the besiegers and so that the enemy would have to divide his forces to blockade each entrance.

Where water was available elaborate use was made of it. Caerphilly is a concentric castle set in the middle of an artificial lake; it is approached by two causeways, one at each side, the ends of which are defended by what are virtually additional castles, each with its own water defences.

The absence of this type of castle in Scotland is probably due to the fact that the King was short of money towards the end of his reign and because many great stone castles, some quite modern, were already in existence. For instance, at Kildrummy in Aberdeenshire, the English added one of their new gatehouses to an already completed fortress.

Chapter Five

The Fourteenth Century

FOURTEENTH-CENTURY ORGANISATION

All the military efforts of Edward II were crippled by the chronic shortage of money which he inherited from his father's reign, and by his own quarrels with the barons over reform of government. His lack of military success, in turn, increased the barons' discontent. The shortage of money meant that, since he could not afford mercenaries, the King had to rely more and more on the unwilling baronage to provide cavalry. His summonses to the militia show that he also required mounted infantry, called 'hobilars', and heavily armoured infantry. By the end of the reign the barons were frequently being called out with all their tenants, as well as the militia raised and led by Arrayers. His continuous demands on the militia and his attempts to increase both their unpaid service and their liability to produce armour, such as hauberks, helmets and iron gauntlets, beyond what was listed in the Statute of Winchester (1285), resulted in their growing resistance to serving.

In the following reign it became so difficult to call up militia for overseas service that the King had to rely more and more on troops raised by contract with his nobles and captains. The beginning of the contract system dates back to shortly after the Conquest, when annual payments were made to knights serving in the King's own household. Fourteenth-century contracts differed only in being purely mercenary without a demand for homage; indeed, many of the contractors were foreigners, like the well-known captain, Sir Walter Manny.

The contractors agreed to serve, usually for a year, with a stated number of followers, at an agreed wage. The force usually consisted of knights, men-at-arms, and infantry – latterly mounted infantry – the majority of whom were archers. The lower ranks were either volunteers or were raised from the militia by the Commissioners of Array especially for the contracted forces. In 1316 the pay of a knight-banneret was four shillings a day, of an ordinary knight two shillings, and of a man-at-arms or squire one shilling.

The system built up a large force of purely professional soldiers of all ranks serving full time and made possible the fighting of prolonged campaigns on the Continent and the permanent garrisoning of captured castles.

The nobility, whose duties throughout the Middle Ages continued to be the support of the King, with advice at all times and with their swords in time of war, remained the natural leaders. Many of the most successful troop contractors were nobles. In 1346 the pay of an Earl was six shillings and eightpence a day; only the Prince of Wales was paid more, at £1 a day. (At the time eggs were twenty-four a penny and chickens two for a penny.)

The militia did not die out but continued in their original role as a formidable force for home defence against Scots, Welsh, or, in coastal districts, against French raiders. Their efficiency was improved, firstly, by a law of 1363 enforcing regular archery practice and, secondly, by numerous efforts to increase their mobility and effectiveness by demands for horses and additional armour from men not required to have them in the past. Parishes began to keep a supply of armour and arms, often stored in the church so that all would know where it could be found in an emergency. Substitutes were demanded of those unable to serve, including the clergy. When the militia were mobilised expenses were paid by the county of ten shillings per head, and the men received royal pay, either from the day they left their home country or from the day they reached the army. This money was raised by a tax, firstly, on those liable to serve but not chosen by the Commissioners and, secondly, on the community as a whole.

In 1346 the pay of the rank and file of the army was: for Esquires, Constables, and Centenars, one shilling a day; for Vintenars, archers on horseback, armoured infantry, and hobilars, sixpence a day; for Vintenars of the Welsh, fourpence a day; for archers, threepence a day; and for Welsh infantry, twopence a day. In addition to this, there was the chance of booty and even a fortune if a soldier managed to capture a noble able to pay a large ransom.

Apart from mounted archers and infantry, Edward III needed knights to serve as officers and to form the backbone of the men-at-arms whether on foot or when acting as cavalry. He was a gallant and chivalrous king, glorying in battle and martial deeds. His personal example helped to popularise the idea of knighthood and he deliberately fostered it by lavish display, by creating knights with great ceremony at feasts such as the Coronation, by his encouragement of knightly sports such as the tournament, and by the foundation of his own chivalric order, the Knights of St George, whose badge was a blue garter inscribed 'Honi soit qui mal y pense' (Evil to him who evil thinks). The emotional attachment to princes found throughout the Middle Ages was sharpened under such a noble king, and all of gentle blood were proud and eager to serve under him. His 'quarrel' with France was personal but affected the honour of his barons and knights. When he ordered a fine on all those who had held land for three years worth £40 a year and who were not yet knights, they came forward readily to be knighted, and it was found that, in any case, the majority of this class were already knights.

The new knightly orders, like the Garter in England and the Star in France, differed from the earlier orders in that they were intended to glorify not God and His service but the King and the chivalric way of life. They usually consisted of a limited number of close friends of the King, bound together by a special oath, taking part in gorgeous ceremonies and elaborate tournaments, in imitation of what were thought to have been the customs of the courts

79

of King Arthur and Charlemagne. A new and very important aspect of chivalry was the romantic feeling for lovely women. The knight was expected to have a beautiful lady whom he admired from afar (at least in theory). Wearing her colours or badge, he would challenge all comers in the tournament to win greater glory for her by his deeds and to gain her admiration. Since the knight was probably already married to another woman for her money or family influence, or because her lands lay near his own, one can see that chivalry was becoming a gigantic game divorced from reality.

O FOURTEENTH-CENTURY TRAINING

The future knight's training in the arts of chivalry began very early. At the age of five he was sent to join the household of the King or some great noble as a page. Here he would learn how to serve his betters, for in the Middle Ages there was nothing undignified in waiting upon a superior; the Black Prince waited at table on his prisoner King John of France. The main subject was behaviour, as good manners were considered of great importance in a knight. The young page would also learn to sing and play music, and his military training soon began with wrestling, fencing with blunt weapons, and, most important of all, horse-mastership, the art of riding and caring for a horse.

It was a harsh age; beatings must have been common, and rough discipline among the pages would have been maintained by the older ones. Slowly the boy would learn to stand on his own feet, to fend for himself, and, by being subjected to discipline, he would learn self-discipline, the most important of all military virtues.

At the age of fourteen the page would expect to become a squire, that is, an apprentice knight. He would continue to wait at his lord's table but he would now also help him put on his armour and would carry his shield and lance on the march. More serious, daily military training would begin, the wearing of armour and practice with weapons. At first he would probably ride with his

The quintain

lance aimed at an old shield on a post. Later he would practise at the 'quintain', a pivoted arm with a target on one end and a weight on the other. When the target was struck the other end of the arm swung round and hit the squire unless he was able to duck quickly or had a good, fast horse to carry him out of reach. Finally, the young squire would practise against his companions. A writer of the time said: 'A youth must have seen his blood flow and felt his teeth crack under the blow of his adversary and have been thrown to the ground twenty times . . . thus will he be able to face real war with the hope of victory.'

The sports used to accustom young soldiers to battle must be nearly as old as war itself. Throughout the Middle Ages there were mimic combats between groups of cavalry, called 'tournaments'; between individual horsemen, known as 'jousts'; or between dismounted men in 'the barriers', the fenced-off arena in which the fight took place. In the eleventh and twelfth centuries the weapons employed were those used in war, and so many lives were lost that successive popes banned the tournament and many of the wiser kings tried to suppress it in their own kingdoms. Richard I, in desperate need of money, sold licences to barons to hold tournaments, a very unwise course to adopt because they were opportunities for barons to meet and to plan revolt. Also, quarrels begun on the tournament field sometimes grew into civil wars.

By the thirteenth century blunt lances were used in some mounted duels, but in others sharp lances were still used. For the tournament held in Windsor Park in 1278, which appears to have been a combat between two groups armed with whalebone swords, the armour bought was of leather. It consisted of chanfrons (helmets for horses), ailettes, body-armours, shields, helms, the last either silvered or gilt according to rank, and, finally, crests.

In the early years of the fourteenth century special armour was developed for the 'joust of peace', that is, the mounted duel with blunt lances. The jousters wore a heavy plate collar, called a 'barber', strapped over the lower part of the front of the helm and coming down on to the breast. The body-armour of small plates

81

The 'joust of peace'. *Above left*, an alternative form of helm

was reinforced with a breastplate which was worn over it. A circular steel plate fitting over the lance protected the right hand. The left hand holding the bridle was protected by a heavy steel gauntlet called the *main-de-fer* (hand of iron). The shield was now often laced to the shoulder to keep it steady. Since blows below the belt were forbidden, leg-armour was not always used. Instead, a heavier saddle with high front and extensions to cover the front of the thighs was employed.

The jousters charged, passing left side to left side so that the shield was towards the opponent. The lance, the head of which had several points to prevent it from actually piercing the armour, was aimed at the opponent across the horse's neck. Points were scored for knocking a man off his horse and for striking off his helm. Breaking a lance also counted, since it could only happen when the blow was struck full on to the centre of the target so that the points did not glance off.

'Jousts of war', that is, with sharp lances, were run in the normal armour for battle, and were often fatal.

In spite of all this stress on military training, the idea that the

Lance Heads for the 'joust of peace'

English medieval aristocracy constantly rode about in full armour is entirely wrong. Many of the gentry took part in the wool trade and occupied themselves with the management of their estates, interesting themselves actively in farm management. The demands of local government gave them little time for military exercises, while hawking by the river with their ladies was less expensive than the tournament. Such knights might pass almost their whole life without putting on the armour they inherited from their father, let alone buying a new one for themselves. Even the sword was not worn in civil life except by travellers.

FOURTEENTH-CENTURY ARMOUR

The first half of the century, in particular, was a time of experiment. There were two probable reasons for this. The growing use of the English longbow on the battlefield made extra protection essential, since mail was no longer sufficient defence. At this time too there was an increasing number of professional soldiers whose whole life was war and who were therefore particularly interested in experiments to find better defences.

The most obvious changes are the widespread use of gutter-shaped plates worn over the mail of the limbs and the appearance of helms with pointed tops. The plates were meant to spread the force of a blow with a sword, axe, or mace and prevent the penetration of an arrow or a sword thrust. The helm was drawn up to a conical point over the crown of the head in order to create a glancing surface away from this most vulnerable point.

The part of the helm covering the face was sometimes made with pivots at the side so that it could be lifted up out of the way when action was not expected; this was called the 'visor'. Some knights who still preferred the steel skull-cap fitted it with a similar visor; others wore the helm, with an open face. All these kinds of headgear were worn over the coif of mail, but by the 'twenties the skull-cap usually had a mail tippet attached to the

Arm defences; early 14th century

83

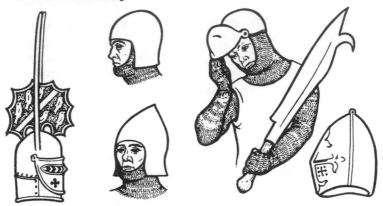

Left, helm of Sir Geoffrey Luttrel about 1340.
Right, helm of William de Staunton about 1326.
Remainder, early 14th century

lower edge and hanging down on to the shoulders. These skull-
caps, called 'basinets', began to be made with a conical top, like
the helm. The helm and the mail tippet of the basinet were fitted
with a quilted lining stuffed with wool or hay.

The gutter-shaped plates were strapped or laced on over the
mail, at first on the outer side of the limbs only. Those worn over
the shins, called the 'greaves', and those worn on the forearms,
were soon hinged to a similar plate so as to enclose the limb entirely. The cup-shaped plates on the elbow and the knee-cap overlapped the other limb plates so as to give the greatest defence at
these points and so that the bending of the limb should not cause a
gap to appear between the plates.

The long gown seems to have been rather a hindrance to the
wearer when on foot and the front part was sometimes tucked up
into the waist-belt. Eventually it was shortened and was made even
shorter at the front than at the back, thus revealing the defences
underneath.

By the 'twenties the well-equipped knight was wearing three
layers of body-armour. Over his shirt he wore the long-sleeved
aketon, over which went his hauberk, and on top of this a body-

84

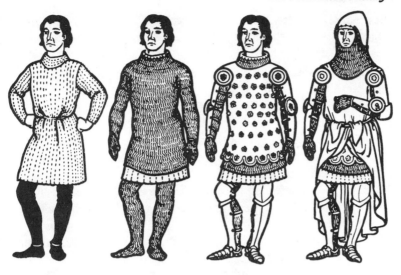

Early fourteenth-century armour showing (left to right)
consecutive layers

armour called 'a pair of plates'. This is actually made of many
small overlapping plates riveted to the inside of a fabric or leather
cover, rather like a scale hauberk turned inside out. The heads of
the rivets can be seen in illustrations below the front edge of the
gown. Sometimes they were made with flower-shaped heads. At
this time probably all the plates were rather small and all of one
size. By the 'forties of this century on the Continent the plates
covering the upper part of the breast had been replaced by a single
plate. Generally, the pair of plates opened down the back and was
put on in the same way as a waistcoat but back-to-front. An assistant would be required to buckle or lace it up the back.

The bag gauntlet of mail remained popular at the beginning of
the century but many illustrations show gauntlets with long stiff
cuffs which contemporary writers tell us are made of whalebone or
steel. The fingers were defended by a series of small half-cylin-

Early fourteenth-century gauntlet and leg armour

85

drical scales, and the knuckles and back of the hand by suitably shaped plates. Like the body-armour these were often riveted to a leather or fabric cover.

Thigh defences are shown on tomb effigies as if quilted and richly embroidered, but they sometimes contained plates, as did those bought for Prince Edward of England for the Scottish campaign of 1302 or 1303. This type remained the most common throughout the greater part of the century. The plates were riveted to a fabric cover and the knee defences were either strapped over them or riveted to them.

The feet were defended by a series of small overlapping plates worn over the mail and presumably allowing the foot to be moved freely inside.

The collar of plates riveted inside a soft cover continued to be worn under the helm and particularly with the kettle-hat.

The bend of the arm and the armpit were often defended by circular plates tied on to the mail at these points.

All these additional defences were expensive, and for the first forty years of the fourteenth century it is quite common for monuments, particularly in the north of England, to show knights wearing very out-of-date equipment, principally mail with only a few plate reinforces. In this age of experiment there was a wide variety of armour to choose from, and some knights clearly preferred mobility to the protection given by an increasing weight of steel.

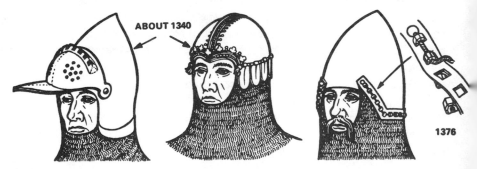

Fourteenth-century basinets

Plate body-armour visible through the lacing of the 'coat armour'; about 1340

By 1346, when the new tactics of the English beat the feudal army of France at Crécy, the conical-topped helm, sometimes with a visor, was worn, occasionally over a basinet. The basinet fitted with its own visor was becoming increasingly popular. It was nearly always conically topped and the visor had a distinct swelling in front of the nose and was sometimes extended downward to protect the throat. The sights were formed by a series of vertical slots cut in a horizontal ridge embossed over each eye; this formed a glancing surface away from the eyes. The mail tippet was sometimes partly covered by a plate collar. The tippet itself could be removed from the helmet for cleaning or repair. The top edge was attached to a leather strip pierced with a series of holes. The holes fitted over staples fixed along the bottom edge of the helmet, and a wire or cord, passed through the staples, then held the two pieces together. In England small plates were often hung from this cord or wire to reinforce the upper part of the tippet.

The gown worn in England, by that time usually called a 'coat armour', was normally sleeveless, tight to the upper part of the body and loose and of equal length around the hips. It was laced up the sides under the arm and in the gaps between the lacings the body-armour was occasionally visible. This usually took the form of a defence made up of horizontal steel hoops riveted inside, or occasionally outside, a leather foundation. A few knights might have a small breastplate like that indicated on the tomb of Sir William Hastings of about 1340, in Abergavenny Church; its central keel can be seen beneath his coat armour. The waist-belt had now been given up but the sword still hung from a diagonal belt with the hilt on the left hip.

A new type of arm defence appeared about this time in which the upper arm was fully enclosed by two plates, while a few narrow horizontal plates overlapped on the shoulder to protect that joint. The elbow defence was linked to plates above and below it by narrow strips of steel, called 'lames'. Each plate would be attached

Gauntlets about 1330–1340

to those above and below it by loosely closed rivets which would allow movement to the joints. Gauntlets now usually had cuffs of plates fitting the forearm closely and strapped round the wrist. Occasionally a bell-shaped cuff with an extension shaped to fit the back of the hand was worn. Ailettes were going out of fashion but had not yet quite disappeared.

Mail horse armour had presumably been found to be too heavy and clumsy, for it is rarely illustrated in this century and is much shorter than before when it does appear. About 1325 one English painting shows a horse with a large shield-shaped plate hung over the front of its head and a crescent-shaped plate hung round its breast from the saddle. The plate horse armour delivered to Edward III in 1338, as he was about to set sail to meet the Emperor Ludwig IV at Coblenz in Germany, probably resembled those on page 82 with the chanfron enclosing the head and fitted with a hinged plate which guarded the top of the neck. Towards the end of the century plate or stiffened leather sheets attached to a suitably shaped piece covering the rump were hung on each side of the horse's hindquarters.

By 1360 the whole breast of the 'pair of plates' often consisted of a single plate, although the skirt was still made of small plates or long narrow horizontal strips so that the wearer could bend. The silhouette of the knight changed a little as a coat armour fitting tightly to the hips became fashionable. Although this was usually simply a heraldic coat, some were quilted like an aketon to give additional protection, such as the coat armour of the Black Prince which is still in Canterbury Cathedral. A few coat armours were actually fixed to the body-armour, and in paintings or monuments hinges can be seen at the join under the arm or on top of the shoulders. The back defence was still made of many small plates but on the Continent the breast and skirt were by now sometimes worn alone and without a cover, being held on by cross-straps over the hauberk at the back.

By the late 1350's a heavy belt, made of jewelled clasps hinged

1. Effigy of John, Earl of Salisbury in Salisbury Cathedral
(1400); his coat armour is apparently fixed to his
body armour. 2. Effigy of Edward, the Black Prince
(1376), Canterbury Cathedral. 3. Brass of Ralph de Knevynton
(1370), Aveley, Essex. 4. Breastplate with straps across the
back

together, was adopted, worn at hip level. It had, apparently, no
practical purpose but was worn by men and women alike in civil
dress, and the sword continued to be worn on the diagonal belt.
Latterly, the sword and dagger were both hung from the hip-belt

on cords or chains, and the belt must have been laced to the coat armour to prevent it from slipping down.

Greaves with backs were almost universal, and the gauntlet with hand and cuff made in one hour-glass-shaped piece of metal replaced the more complicated earlier form. Until they were required the gauntlets could be buttoned together and hung over the hilt of the sword.

The defence of the knee, called the 'poleyn', had a small wing to guard the bend of the limb. A similar wing appeared at the elbow. The monument to the Black Prince, who died in 1376, shows the new fashion of leg-armour with a plate thigh defence with a hinged side plate to cover the outside of the leg. The poleyn is linked to the defences above and below by narrow lames, and the foot, completely enclosed in narrow, overlapping plates, is drawn to a sharp point like the contemporary civilian shoe. A horizontal rib of steel was sometimes riveted across the top of the thigh defence to prevent a weapon sliding over the edge and into the groin.

In the early part of the century the tippet of mail had fitted fairly closely to the neck; now it was much fuller, flowing out on to the points of the shoulders, probably due to increased padding in the lining. It was often tied or buckled down to the coat armour to prevent a weapon getting underneath.

The basinet became first rather egg-shaped and then very pointed. Those of the nobility were often encircled by a jewelled wreath or coronet. The front of the visor was drawn out to a sharp point to provide a glancing surface over the face. The vision and breathing slots were placed at the crest of ridges so that a weapon point could not slide into them off the surface of the visor. Since the left side, the shield side, was if possible always kept towards the enemy, that side of the visor was made without breaths so as not to weaken it.

By the 1380's a small bracket was often attached to the breastplate on the right side. A steel or leather ring was fixed round the lance just behind the handgrip. When couching the lance beneath the arm the rim of this circle was pressed against the bracket on the breastplate. When the lance struck its target the blow was

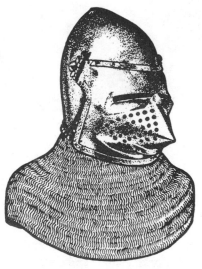

Basinet and mail tippet (aventail) of about 1390, from
Churburg in South Tyrol. (Now in the Tower of
London)

taken by the bracket and the armour, so that the hand was not
forced back under the arm. Although this bracket is not illustrated
in England in this century, it is shown on French tomb effigies.

Richly decorated armour studded with pearls and precious
stones is described in poetry and the inventories of castles and
princes. All these have long vanished but a few bits of armour of
this period have survived with silver or gilt-brass decorative edges
engraved with flowers, fleurs-de-lis, and interlace. Some have
religious or romantic inscriptions.

Armours did not have pockets, but money and small possessions
were carried in a pouch attached to the belt as in civil dress.

By the end of the century the recognised badge of the English
soldier was the red cross of St George on a white ground; this
was worn either covering his jacket or forming a distinctive part
of it.

Until the fourteenth century the spur was simply a Y-shaped

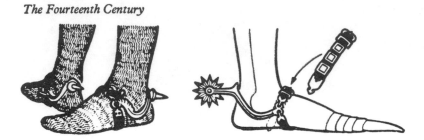

Left, prick spur, late-thirteenth century.
Right, rowel spur (1376)

frame strapped round the heel, the stem of which consisted of a spike that could be jabbed into the horse. To prevent it from sticking in too far the spike was shaped like a pyramid, or swelled out into a ball about half an inch from the point. At the beginning of the fourteenth century the single spike was replaced by a star-shaped wheel revolving on an axle fitted into the stem of the Y. Since it is more difficult to stick in several spikes than one, this type was probably less cruel than the earlier spur.

FOURTEENTH-CENTURY ARMS

Sword blades were of very varied types; some were purely for thrusting, others were designed so that they could be used for both cutting and thrusting. Many knights carried a thrusting sword hung on the front of their saddle, as well as the dual-purpose sword on the hip-belt. The exclusive thrusting sword had a stiff blade of diamond cross-section tapering from the hilt to the point, which was sometimes reinforced for piercing. The blade of the dual-purpose sword was usually wide near the hilt and sharp on both sides but tapered to a very sharp point for thrusting. One sometimes reads that the medieval sword was a clumsy weapon, blunt and unwieldy. No one who had ever held a genuine sword in his hand could say that, since they feel so perfectly designed for their purpose as soon as one's hand closes round the grip. The few still in their original condition are very sharp indeed. Many blades were a good deal longer than formerly, and, to balance the extra weight, the grip was also made longer and the pommel was often of elongated shape as well. In order to get a better grip when thrusting, the first finger was sometimes hooked over the front bar of the cross-guard, and so that this finger should not get cut, a short section of the blade was occasionally made with a thick un-sharpened edge, later called the 'ricasso'. The grip was bound with wire or string to prevent the hand slipping. Many swords had a leather or metal flap at the centre of the cross-guard which prevented rain from running down inside the scabbard. A wet scabbard would soon ruin a blade by rusting it and the sword might even become jammed in the scabbard by rusting.

The cross-guard was usually straight or slightly curved towards the blade. During the first three-quarters of the century the sword and the dagger and often the helm were attached to the armour of the knight's chest by long chains so that they did not get lost in battle, see page 89.

The fashion for fighting on foot made the long-handled axe

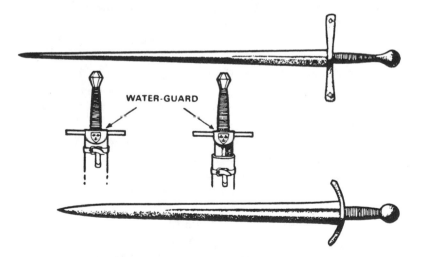

WATER-GUARD

Above, thrusting sword, about 1400.
Below, dual-purpose sword, early 14th century

Early fourteenth-century axe

popular as a knightly weapon. The extra leverage of the long shaft made it more deadly than shorter axes, and the dismounted knight had both hands free to use it. The lance, cut down to five foot to make it more wieldy, was used on foot but was found to be less effective than the axe at close quarters. Eventually, the two weapons were combined by putting a spear-like spike on the upper end of the axe shaft.

Short axes, hammers with a rear spike, and the mace remained popular for mounted combats and were carried hanging on the front of the saddle. The mace became the typical weapon of the King's Sergeants-at-Arms, and illustrations of the period show them carried by Royal guards. Since they were carried by Royal officers, they became badges of authority and are now used to show the authority of courts of law from the House of Commons down.

The ordinary soldier often used a long-shafted bill-hook with a spike, not found on the agricultural tool, on the top, and this became one of the characteristic weapons of the English infantry.

The decisive weapon of the English archers, the longbow, made of the wood of yew, elm, ash, or wychelm, was the full height of the wielder. It was usually tipped at each end with cowhorn grooved to take the linen string. When not in use the bow was stored unstrung in a bag. The archer gripped his weapon with the left hand about the middle, where it was some four and a half inches round, and, holding back the string with the first two fingers of the right hand, he forced the centre of the bow away from him, thus bending it. The secret of the longbow was constant practice from childhood with bows to match the growing strength of the boy. Practice was compulsory and took place on Sundays and holidays, usually beside the village church. Many an English church can still show the grooves in the stones of the porch which are said to have been made by bowmen sharpening their arrows.

Ash or birch woods were used by the fletchers (from the French

Mid fourteenth-century axe

94

Fourteenth-century mace and bill

word for an arrow – *flèche*) who made the arrows. They were thirty to thirty-six inches long, with three flights made of grey goose feathers. Chaucer's Yeoman had arrows with peacock feathers, but Roger Ascham, tutor to Queen Elizabeth I and a famous authority on archery, thought these a great vanity. The head of the arrow was steel, at first fairly broad, but later examples designed to pierce plate armour, or to find its joints, were more acutely pointed. The extreme range of the longbow was over 400 yards. By a statute of Henry VIII no one over twenty-four years of age might practise at a range of less than 220 yards.

The inside of the archer's wrist was protected from the snap of the bowstring by a 'bracer', a piece of horn, leather, or bone strapped inside the wrist.

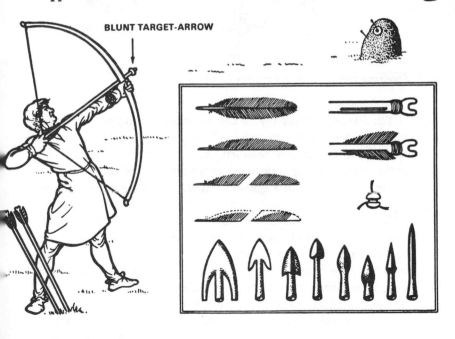

BLUNT TARGET-ARROW

Archery practice at the butts

Spanning and shooting a windlass crossbow

The arrows were usually carried in a bunch of twenty-four stuck through a loop in the waist-belt. The Scots, who had a great respect for the southern bowmen, had a saying: 'Every English archer carries twenty four Scots under his belt'. Mounted archers carried their shafts in a quiver attached to the right side of the saddle.

The Lowland Scots never had many bowmen in spite of laws banning football and golf and ordering regular practice with the bow on pain of the fine of a sheep from all those who failed to do so. The French relied on the crossbow, now a more powerful weapon requiring a windlass with pulleys and cords to bend it. The disadvantage of the crossbow was the length of time required to span it, which gave it a slower rate of fire than the longbow and meant that each crossbowman required a second soldier carrying a large rectangular shield about five foot high to give him shelter while reloading. It has been said that the absence of these shields at Crécy caused the disastrous failure of the Genoese crossbowmen on that day. They were not expecting to have to fight, and the shields were on the baggage carts far to the rear. The advantages of the crossbow were that it required neither great strength nor long practice to use it. The rate of fire could be increased when defending a castle by stationing two bowmen at each loophole.

The arrows used were shorter and thicker than those used for the longbow and were 'feathered' with leather or thin wooden flights. It was found that if the flights were fixed on diagonally the arrow spun in flight and kept a much straighter course. This was the system later adopted for the rifle. The quarrels were carried point upwards in a quiver on the waist-belt.

By the end of the fourteenth century the French had organised a considerable force of native crossbowmen by the foundation of corporations of crossbowmen in each of the chief towns. These were originally meant only to defend their own walls but were later called out to join the field army, when they were paid and supplied by the King.

THE BEGINNING OF GUNS

During the second quarter of the fourteenth century a new weapon appeared which was eventually to make armour obsolete. This was the gun. Roger Bacon, the Franciscan scholar, writing in the 1260's, mentions gunpowder as being already quite well known in many lands as a child's toy. In one of his later writings it is clear that he foresaw its destructive force as a bomb but not as a driving force for bullets. Bacon and others probably gained their knowledge from Arabic writings, since saltpetre, the essential ingredient, had been known in the East for some time. Many recipes were tried throughout the Middle Ages and the Renaissance but the commonest fourteenth-century one is four parts of saltpetre to one of carbon and one part of sulphur. These are ground up fine with pestle in a mortar, and well mixed. No one today believes the old

97

story that gunpowder was invented by Berthold Scharz, a German monk.

The first undoubted reference to guns is an order by the Council of Florence, in 1326, to prepare iron bullets and cannon of metal for the defence of the Republic. At the same time an illuminated manuscript made for Edward III by his chaplain, Walter de Milemete, illustrates a cannon being fired. The curious bottle shape may be so that the portion where the gunpowder actually exploded was strongest. The inside of the barrel was probably cylindrical like a modern gun and like a very early bottle-shaped gun which

18 INCHES

Left, Walter de Milemete's gun, 1326–7
Right, bronze gun excavated at Loshult, Sweden (National Historical Museum, Stockholm)

has survived. The gun in the manuscript is coloured gold and was probably of cast brass. Casting a brass gun would have been a simple task for the foundry that made the very beautiful effigies of Henry III and his queen in Westminster Abbey, and cast guns are certainly mentioned in France in 1345. Milemete shows the gun lying on a table without any visible method of attachment. In reality, it would probably have to be lashed down or held down by metal bands to prevent it recoiling backwards and perhaps killing the gunner.

Rather surprisingly, the gun in the manuscript is firing an arrow, but many accounts and chroniclers describe arrows for guns. Presumably a wad would have to be placed between the powder and the back of the arrow to push it out. The gunner is firing his piece with what is, probably, a burning cord or stick

98

at the end of a short holder, which he had put into a small touch-hole on top of the barrel near the back leading down into the powder. The 'feathers' for gun-arrows were made of brass. Stone and lead balls were both used in the fourteenth century.

From this simple type of gun, artillery developed rapidly. By 1377 a gun firing a ball of 200 pounds used at the siege of Ardres is mentioned by Froissart. A gun of this size was probably not cast but was built up of strips of iron like many surviving guns of the fifteenth century. These were made like an old-fashioned wooden beer-barrel: long strips of iron were built into a cylinder, probably around a wooden core, and were held in place by hoops of iron. The hoops were made exactly the right size and were then heated to expand them so that they could be slipped over the barrel. On cooling, the hoops would contract, gripping the bars tightly. The whole thing would then be heated as fiercely as possible to weld the metal together and to burn out the core. Since the resultant tube was open at both ends, one end was closed by an iron chamber for the powder. In the smaller guns this would be loaded with powder and wedged into the breech behind the ball, and these were true breech-loaders. In the larger guns it is obvious that the chamber would be much too heavy to remove for each shot. In any case, illustrations show these big guns being fired lying on the ground in specially built frames which would prevent the removal of the breech-block. They must therefore be muzzle-loaders. In this type the front part of the breech-block was made narrower than

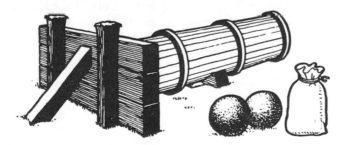

A large gun in position and ready to fire

99

TOUCH-HOLE

7½ INCHES

A late fourteenth-century handgun (National Historical
Museum, Stockholm)

the back part and slid inside the barrel. The frame around the back
of the gun would prevent the chamber being blown out by the
kick of the explosion. The powder was fired through a hole bored
in the top of the chamber.

In 1364 the town of Perugia in Italy bought 500 small guns
which could be carried in the hand, and in 1386 'handguns' are
mentioned in the English Royal Accounts for the first time. Surviving handguns of this time have short brass barrels with a socket
at the rear for a wooden shaft. They were fired by a touch-hole
exactly like the full-sized guns.

Italian writers of the time excuse the failure of the Genoese at
Crécy by saying that they were thrown into confusion by the
English guns. Edward III certainly owned guns at the time of the
battle and used them the next year at the siege of Calais but no one
knows for certain whether they were really used at Crécy. Guns
played little part in battles until the following century, and even in
sieges catapults, balistas, trebuchets, and mining sheds were still
used alongside guns.

T TACTICS AND STRATEGY IN THE FOURTEENTH CENTURY

The fourteenth century saw the rise of the English from an obscure
island people to the first soldiers in Europe. For fifty years they

suffered no major defeat, and any foreign army with even a few English mercenaries was sure of victory.

The English had been crushingly defeated by the Scots at Bannockburn in 1314, when their archers had been swept out of the field by the small cavalry reserve of the Scots, just as they were coming into action. The English knights and men-at-arms, all mounted, broke like waves on the granite rocks of the Scottish spearmen. At Halidon Hill in 1333 the English copied the Scots by all dismounting and taking up a defensive position on a hill, men-at-arms and archers mixed together. The Scots were forced to attack them because they needed to relieve Berwick, which the English were besieging. Dismounting, the Scots charged up the hill and were shot down by the English archers without ever coming to grips with the men-at-arms.

During Edward III's wars with the French these tactics were developed for use against the feudal cavalry of France. It would have been impossible for Edward to fight the French with a conventional feudal army of cavalry. The knighthood of France far outnumbered that of England and when two cavalry charges meet, other things being equal, it is numbers that count. The English men-at-arms and knights therefore dismounted and formed up, usually in three lines, two in front and one in reserve. The archers were drawn up in wedge-shaped blocks on the ends of the front lines. The ground was always carefully chosen so that the flanks were protected by woods or villages through which cavalry could not attack. The front was, if possible, protected by a hedge and faced downhill so that the enemies' charge was slowed down and the advantage of additional height was given to the English.

At first, as at Crécy in 1346, the French answered these tactics by a cavalry charge directed against the men-at-arms, usually without any attempt to reconnoitre the English position. As a result, before they ever came to blows, many hundreds were shot down and the remainder were bunched together in an uncontrollable mass as they shrank away from the arrows of the archers on the wings. The survivors were easily flung back by the rock steadiness of the English men-at-arms. At Crécy, where the first attack was made without orders from the French King, no fewer than fifteen attacks were made by new waves of the French as they arrived on the field.

Later, misreading the lesson of Crécy, the French also dismounted, but they charged on foot in exactly the same fashion and with identical results. The English were able to vary their tactics to suit each situation. At Poitiers, in 1356, the Black Prince kept ready a small cavalry reserve. The first French attack was mounted; the second division attacked on foot and was only fought off with great difficulty; the last division, led by the French King in person, was long delayed, and the appearance on the field of a huge body of fresh troops, just when the English had had their fill of fighting for one day and had run out of arrows, must have been very disheartening. The Prince, realising that things were desperate, seized the initiative. Ordering up the horses and remounting his men, he led a furious charge down the slope at the dismounted enemy. At the same time he slammed in the cavalry reserve in a right hook to the French rear. The enemy resisted strongly but at length broke and fled, leaving their King and 2,000 knights and men-at-arms as prisoners.

Edward III was well aware of the difficulty of defeating France, with its population so much greater than that of England. He therefore tried two strategies. The first was used when the aim was merely to defeat France in order to regain the English lands in Gascony seized by the French King. Gascony was a long and very uncertain sea voyage from England; on the other hand, near at hand lay Flanders, traditionally friendly to England because of the wool trade and now in revolt against its French count. Attack through Flanders, in alliance with the Flemish burghers and his wife's kinsmen, including the Emperor of Germany, would make the French recall their troops from Gascony to defend Paris. This system, in which England with its wealth acted as paymasters for numerous allies, was to be used in many later wars on the Continent. On this occasion the allies proved faithless, and the expense too great. The only important event was the naval battle of Sluys in 1340 which for a time gave England command of the Channel and the trade routes to Flanders.

Edward's second strategy was aimed at conquering France. Each of his great campaigns was planned to be fought on three fronts so as to divide the numerically vastly superior French army. For instance, the Crécy campaign of 1346 was part of a complex plan which included not only Edward's invasion of Normandy, which was to be supported by a Flemish force advancing to meet him from the north-east, but also campaigns by the Earl of Derby in Gascony in the south-west and by Sir Thomas Dagworth in Brittany in the north-west. The French army at Crécy vastly outnumbered the English, but the situation would have been much grimmer if the other large French army pinned down in Gascony had been free to join them.

The reason for the success of the English, often operating far from their bases and invariably outnumbered, lies as much in the organisation of their army as in their tactics and strategy. The army consisted of trained professional soldiers commanded by officers in whom the men had confidence. Co-operation in local government at home had built up respect between the classes making up the army. Long service together increased both their efficiency and that 'band of brothers' feeling throughout all ranks, which makes soldiers stand together in moments of crisis. Victory after victory added to their morale and made them feel invincible. They did not fear to attack the French even when outnumbered by them four to one as at Roche Derrien in 1347.

The French army, on the other hand, continued to be purely feudal; it consisted mainly of feudal cavalry, well-disciplined mercenary crossbowmen, usually Genoese, and the infantry of the levy. The last, since selective service was unknown, were of little use and rarely played an important part in battles. The feudal cavalry made up the greater part of the army. They usually showed great courage but were without discipline or central organisation. At Crécy they opened the battle without orders and without waiting for the reserves to close up. At Poitiers King John seems to have been completely out of touch with his leading divisions. Their continual lack of success lowered French morale and led them to expect only defeat.

After Poitiers the French refused to meet the English in the field, and retired into fortresses and towns, allowing their enemies to march to and fro across France. Only when the coast was clear would the French commander, Duguesclin, slip out to recapture castles along the borders. In the end, time and growing French nationalism were to win back almost all Edward's conquests.

FOURTEENTH-CENTURY CASTLES

After the building of the great Royal fortresses in Wales the importance of castles declined in England. Because the strength of these new strongholds made sieges unprofitable campaigns were usually conducted with large field armies fighting pitched battles. Individual barons were no longer powerful enough to revolt; the later struggles were between the King and combinations of barons able to raise large forces to meet the Royal army in the open field.

The few completely new castles built in this century, such as Bodiam in Sussex, intended to protect the coast against French raiders, retained the four-square plan of the thirteenth century,

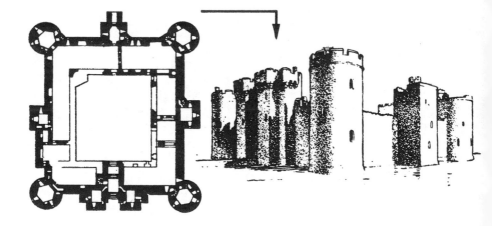

Bodiam (1383)

with corner towers and a large gatehouse modelled on those at Beaumaris. Bodiam stands in a large artificial lake and has a gate defended by two drawbridges and an island outwork linked to the shore by a long wooden bridge. In castles such as this, where a strong garrison of mercenary troops, whose loyalty might sometimes be in doubt, was always in residence, the strong point, the gatehouse, was usually the captain's quarters and was separated from the garrison so that if the troops mutinied he could hold out against them with his personal retainers.

One of the problems facing the defenders of a castle had always been how to drop missiles on miners working at the foot of the wall without exposing themselves to the enemy archers. In the late thirteenth century this was overcome by building the parapet of the wall-walk on a series of stone brackets jutting out from the outer face of the wall. Stones, sharpened logs, and incendiaries could be dropped through the gaps between the brackets, down the outer face of the wall from behind the cover provided by the wall top. In England this was used mainly on gatehouses.

Special openings were now built into castles so that the defenders could use small guns. These usually consisted of round holes at the bottom of the loophole, which now began to look like a keyhole upside down. The gun was fixed to a movable beam which lay on the floor inside the wall, level with the hole.

The increasing demand for a luxurious life and the decreasing military importance of castles led to them being built more for comfort than for defence. The internal buildings surrounded the whole square of the courtyard and were now built in one with the walls. External windows were made larger, and towers lower. In the south of England castles continued to be built, probably because of the growing romantic interest in chivalry – the harking back to the Golden Age of King Arthur and the Knights of the Round Table – and because great barons felt they must have a

Fourteenth-century gun-port

Hurstmonceaux (1440)

castle as the central residence of their estates for reasons of prestige. In the following century this resulted in the building of fairy-tale castles like Hurstmonceaux (1440), complete with moat, towers, and wall top built out on brackets but all made of thin brickwork.

In the north of England, where the country was poor and therefore the baronage was also poor, and the danger from a foreign foe, the Scots, very real, true castles were still being built. These were not the expensive and complicated concentric castles but a continuation of the old motte-and-bailey idea. A strong tower replaced the motte, and instead of the bailey there was a courtyard with high walls within which a man could lock up his family and cattle until the raiders were gone.

The majority of the castles which we see all over these Islands were not built at one time and so do not fit into any of the types discussed so far. The plan of many castles was affected by the site on which they were built. Edinburgh Castle on its great crag is an example: the outer walls are placed on the very edge of a precipice on every side except the front, where a great gun battery covers the approach. Most castles developed by the addition of extra defences or accommodation as these became fashionable or necessary, or if and when the owner could afford them.

Caerlaverock in Dumfriesshire is a splendid example of a castle

Caerlaverock

which has developed: it is triangular in plan with large circular towers at two corners, and two, with the gate between them, on the third corner, and it is surrounded by a moat. Although it was partly demolished several times by the English and Scots in the following century, a poem of 1300 shows that it was already like this then. In the late fifteenth century new battlements were built out on brackets on the tops of the towers, a short outerwork was built between the gate towers and new rooms built on to the back of them, and finally a range of rooms was built inside one of the curtain walls. In the late sixteenth century horizontal gunports were made in the towers and, probably at the same time, the earth bank outside the moat was raised and strengthened, partly to protect the base of the walls from gunfire and partly to form emplacements for artillery too heavy to mount on the walls. In 1634 an elegant series of buildings in the Renaissance style was built along the other two sides of the courtyard, and large windows made in the outer walls. The castle fell to the Covenanters in 1640, after holding out for thirteen weeks, and was never afterwards used as the residence of its lord.

Chapter Six

The Fifteenth Century

0 THE FIFTEENTH-CENTURY ARMY (LIVERY AND MAINTENANCE)

The troops for the French war continued to be raised by contract as before, and Parliament began to have some control over the free companies, as the contract troops were called, absence without leave becoming a criminal offence punishable by law. The great feudal landowners were still the leaders and the most efficient contractors, as well as acting as Commissioners of Array of the militia for home defence. The militia was used effectively for campaigns both in Wales and in Scotland, and was called out by Richard III in his last campaign. Pay, clothes, and arms were supplied by the community, and at least one English church still contains arms and armour for the contingent of the village. The levy in the late fifteenth century included billmen and handgunners as well as archers and spearmen. While at one time the bulk of the archers came from country districts, the encouragement of archery practice over a long period meant that the forces of the largest towns now also included many efficient bowmen.

The contract system was ideal for long campaigns overseas but in time of peace was extremely dangerous for the King, impoverished as he was by the war. The end of the war in France brought home a large number of unemployed professional soldiers, eager to take the pay of some great baron and bored by the humdrum life of peaceful England. The great landowners tended to keep private armies for reasons of prestige and because it was traditional for them to do so. The King, without a standing army of his own, was only able to retaliate against a disloyal baron by using the armies of those barons who remained loyal. This undoubtedly weakened him in the eyes of his baronage and led, among other things, to the decline in the authority of his courts of law. This, together with a sharp decline in the Church's hold on men's minds, led to corruption and intimidation in the administration of justice. Since justice was no longer obtainable by fair means, the yeomanry and smaller gentry sought the protection of one of the great landowners. They would wear his badge and livery and maintain him in his quarrels in return for his protection in theirs. (Livery in this case means a coat of heraldic colours.) Service to some great noble might mean advancement to rank and wealth faster and more surely than honest work. To the great landowner himself the help of the lesser men was important, since, in a period when his love of costly display and expensive sports clashed with rising prices and an agricultural depression, he must constantly struggle to increase his wealth and authority. The system became known as 'Livery and Maintenance'.

The courts were further weakened as the system developed. Now, if a Royal judge could not be bribed he could be intimidated by the sight of a crowd of armed men hanging about the courthouse and wearing the badge of one of the parties in the case. Sometimes it would be impossible to find a jury whose allegiance was not already given to one of the lords in the trial. Finally, during the long regency of Henry vi's reign justice largely collapsed; even the Royal judges openly broke the law; and the barons began to settle their quarrels by war against each other, thus preparing the way for the Wars of the Roses.

The armies of these wars were formed largely from the retainers, contract troops, and dependants of the great barons. This type of force could be rapidly called together and was relatively cheap, since most of those wearing livery were unpaid. Paid soldiers usually fight well but when the reward of victory is personal advancement and wealth the soldier fights even better. In moments of great need both sides used Commissions of Array to call out the militia on pain of imprisonment or even death.

Acts against Livery and Maintenance were widely ignored throughout the fifteenth century, and it was not until Henry Tudor ascended the throne in 1485 that the huge bodies of retainers and supporters could be suppressed. By that time the greater part of the baronage was dead on the battlefield or the block, and the country as a whole was sick of war and longing for a strong government. It was the memory of this long period of bloodshed that enabled the despotic Tudors to reign almost unopposed. They were able to suppress baronial armies and to make artillery a royal monopoly. On the whole, their guns were sufficient deterrent against revolt.

A number of English kings, including Edward III, Richard II, and Edward IV, had permanent bodyguards of archers in addition to the Knights and Sergeants of the Royal Household. The Yeomen of the Guard, who now guard the Sovereign on state occasions, are the direct descendants of the guard of archers raised by Henry VII in 1485, consisting of fifty yeomen under a captain.

FIFTEENTH-CENTURY SOLDIERS

The first years of the fifteenth century saw the suit of plate armour completed by the adoption of a backplate to match the breastplate, and by the general adoption of two or more gorget plates worn over the mail tippet of the basinet. The helmet became more rounded and, by the 'twenties, fitted closely to the contours of the head. The pointed visor remained popular but one with a blunt swelling over the nose and mouth became more usual. The lower edge of the visor, when closed, fell inside the upper edge of the gorget plate so that no weapon could catch under it and force open the visor.

Although paintings depict many knights wearing heraldic tunics, most English monuments show armour without any covering. The front half of the body-armour was hinged to the back part down the

Gorget plates of the basinet

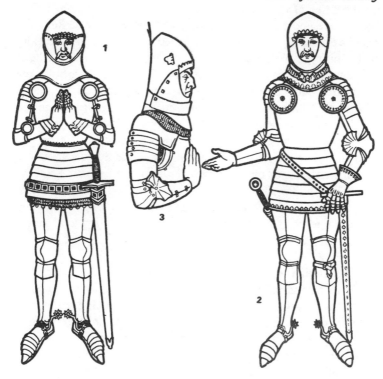

1. Brass of Sir Ivo Fitzwaryn, died 1414. 2. Brass of
Lord Camoys, K.G. died 1419. He commanded the English left wing
at Agincourt. 3. Effigy of Alexander Stewart, Earl of Buchan,
carved about 1420

left side under the arm and closed by straps and buckles down the
right side. The back and breast were closed across the shoulders
by more buckles and straps. The skirt, made of horizontal hoops
of steel, hung from the breast and back by straps inside the metal
and was hinged and buckled at the sides.

The gap at the armhole, necessary to allow the arms to move
freely, was protected by a small plate, usually round or rectangular,
hanging down on a strap from the shoulder defence. From the
1430's this plate was sometimes made in one with the plate cover-

ing the point of the shoulder, which was now made deeper than those above and below it. The wings of the elbow and knee defences were either heart-shaped or fluted and shaped like a cockleshell. This type of armour is still shown on brasses of the middle of the century and armours like these would have been worn by the better-equipped knights and men-at-arms at Agincourt in 1415.

Wills and inventories sometimes mention armours imported from overseas; armour of Lombardy (North Italy) was particularly popular, as well as swords of Cologne, Milan, and Savoy. No doubt merchants trading abroad would include a few armours in their mixed cargoes on the return journey. Indeed, in Scotland they had to by law. From about 1440 some English brasses illustrate armours in the Italian fashion. In 1441 an English captain, Sir John Cressy, is known to have bought a ready-made Milanese armour for £8 6s. 8d., while the armour for a squire cost from £5 to £6 16s. 8d.

These Italian armours differ from those already described, mainly in having large shoulder defences curving round to cover part of the breast and back with additional reinforcing plates over the front of each; there was also a reinforce on the large wing of the right elbow and a large reinforcing plate covering the left elbow; shield-shaped guards, called 'tassets', were hung from the bottom of the skirt to cover the top of the thighs. The wings of the knee defences and elbows now curved round to give as much protection as possible to the inside of the joint. The right shoulder defence and its reinforce were shaped to allow room for the lance to be couched under the arm. In order to allow as much freedom of movement as possible, the breast- and backplate were divided horizontally, the lower part overlapping the upper part and being strapped to it. The lance-rest on these Italian armours was a steel bracket attached to the breastplate by staples.

A new type of gauntlet came in, much stronger and safer than the earlier one. The cuff was longer and pointed, and the fingers were protected by two or three heavy lames lying across their

Lance-rest of Italian type

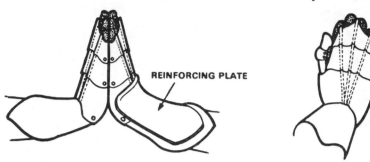

English gauntlets, about 1435

backs. These were worn either over bare hands or with leather gloves inside.

The plate shoe was shaped like the fashionable pointed shoe of the day and consisted of a large number of narrow overlapping strips of steel allowing the foot to move freely. A single plate hinged to the side of the front part enclosed the heel. To give a surer footing the spurs and steel shoes were usually removed for fighting on foot.

The strength of armour was now so much improved that the shield became unnecessary for the knight but, as a precaution, the reinforcing plates for the left arm, which remained motionless grasping the reins, were heavier and larger than those on the right. In England, a single heavy plate, suitably shaped to cover the back of the hand, was sometimes worn to reinforce the left gauntlet.

English knights seem to have preferred to wear the well-tried basinet and gorget plates with the new fashion of armour. Usually the back of the helmet was made to come down on to the backplate, where it was secured by a strap and buckle; the face-opening had a horseshoe-shaped plate around the lower edge, overlapped by the front gorget plate, which again was strapped to the breast. Italian armourers made their export models with this type of helmet and other modifications to suit their foreign customers.

The theory of the glancing surface has been mentioned before. The Italian armourers carried it a little further. A diagonal rib

113

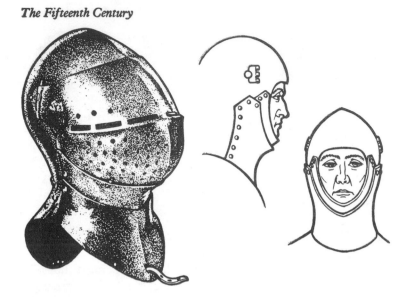

Basinets; *far left*, about 1450; *right*, about 1435, front and side view

was hammered up across the shoulder reinforces to lead a point away from the throat, and the upper edge of these reinforces was turned out to form a second deflecting surface. The edge of the breastplate, at the neck and the armholes, was rolled outwards to form a strong raised rim to prevent a weapon sliding over the edge. The top edge of the thighs was treated in the same way. Additional ribs of steel were riveted on the forearms to prevent a point sliding up into the joints of the elbow defence; others were fitted to the backs of the shoulder defences. As time went on the lower half of the breastplate overlapped more and more of the upper part, finally covering it almost completely and acting as a reinforce.

A fine example of one of these Milanese armours appears on the monument of Richard Beauchamp, Earl of Warwick, at Warwick, which was made in about 1450, 'armed according to patterns' as the contract for making it says. The figure was cast in the round,

Raised rim at top of thigh, about 1450

114

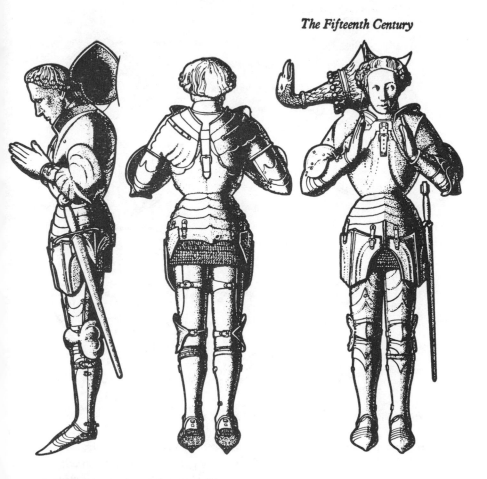

Effigy of the Earl of Warwick, about 1450, showing an
Italian armour

so the back of the armour is also illustrated. Instead of the usual
basinet, the Earl's helmet, which lies under his head, is an armet,
a small headpiece fitting closely to the head and completely
enclosing it.

The 'armet' consisted of a hemispherical skull, hinged to which
were two side-plates locking together at the chin. The joint of these
two plates, at the rear, was protected by a narrow tail extending

115

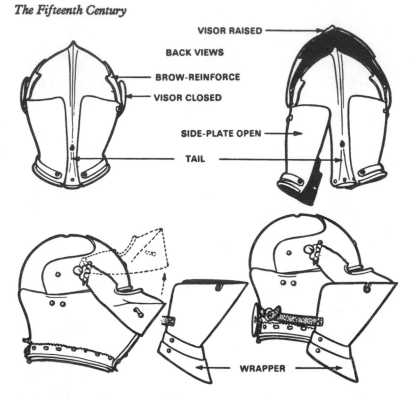

VISOR RAISED

BACK VIEWS

BROW-REINFORCE

VISOR CLOSED

SIDE-PLATE OPEN

TAIL

WRAPPER

Armets; above, about 1500; below, about 1470

downwards from the skull. A small pointed visor fell over the side-plates. The wearer saw out of a narrow gap between the top edge of the visor and the lower edge of the skull. The brow was reinforced by an additional plate, the bottom of which was rolled outwards to form a stop-rib over the eyes. The upper edge of the visor was similarly rolled outwards to form a rib below the sight. A small mail tippet was attached to the lower edge of the helmet to defend the neck; the front was covered by an additional plate, called a 'wrapper', shaped like the bow of a ship, which strapped round the neck and had one or two gorget plates. The straps of this plate were supported by a pin projecting from the tail of the skull and were defended by a steel disc on the end of a pin.

In the meantime a different style of armour was being developed in Germany. While Italian armours were rounded and smooth with simple and large surfaces in the Renaissance style, those of Germany were spiky and broken in outline and surface in keeping with northern Gothic fashions. The surface of most of the plates was decorated with a group of radiating flutes, and wherever a flute reached the edge of a plate the metal was drawn out into a point. Usually the number of plates was greater than in Italian armours, and even the breastplate was divided into three or more pieces with sharp points running up the central keel. The arm defences were each made in three separate parts: the two tubes, one for the upper arm, the other for the forearm, and a large guard for the elbow. These were tied on to the aketon by laces, those on the elbow being visible outside the plate as two bows. The earlier light shoulder defence, with its small plate hanging over the armhole, remained the most popular. The lance-rest was a light bracket bolted to the breastplate and could be hinged out of the way when not required.

Trade routes from Germany and Italy met in the Low Countries, and many armourers from Italy worked in the cities of Flanders. Here the two fashions of armour blended: the plates were usually fluted and rather spiky in the German fashion but tassets and shoulder reinforces in the Italian fashion were common.

Armours of this type are also illustrated in many English monuments from the middle of the century. These may represent armours made in England or armours imported by the many English merchants trading in the Low Countries. English knights often wore their tassets strapped on halfway up the skirt rather than on the lower edge, and they sometimes also wore large tassets at the sides and even at the back. The usual helmet worn with this type of armour was a development of the kettle-hat and was called a 'salet'. The back of the brim was drawn down into a pointed tail to give greater protection to the neck. The front was made deeper to cover the upper part of the face, and pierced with a horizontal slit so that the wearer could see out. Usually the front part, including the sight, was pivoted as a visor and could be pushed up out of

117

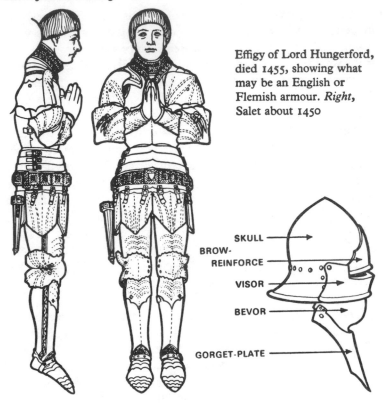

Effigy of Lord Hungerford, died 1455, showing what may be an English or Flemish armour. *Right*, Salet about 1450

SKULL

BROW-REINFORCE

VISOR

BEVOR

GORGET-PLATE

the way until battle commenced. The neck and the lower part of the face were normally protected by a bevor strapped round the neck. Occasionally the mail coif was still worn under the salet. Flemish and English salets very often have pointed tops to the skulls.

It was in armours of the Italian and the Flemish fashion that the English knighthood fought the Wars of the Roses.

Whether the knight was preparing for battle or for tournament he would require the help of his squire to put on his armour. He would first put on an aketon, which would have suitably shaped pieces of mail tied on under the arms and inside the bend of the elbow by means of strong waxed-cord arming-laces. These pieces

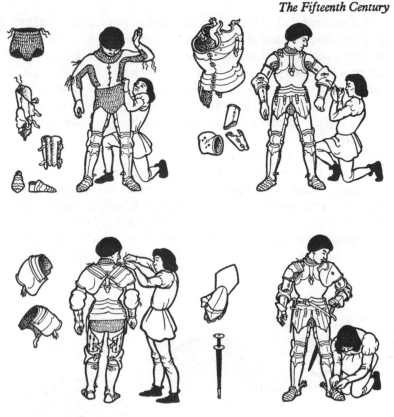

Arming a knight, about 1450

of mail defended parts of the body not fully protected by plates. Round his neck the knight would wear a collar of mail. He would also put on a pair of hose (i.e. tights) with padding around the knees to protect them from the pressure of the leg-armour. Over these would be a pair of stout leather shoes fitted with arming-laces: these were to tie on the plate shoes which were the first parts of the armour to be put on. The greaves, made in two halves hinged vertically down the outside of the calf, were then buckled on, followed by the thigh defences and knee-pieces, which again strapped around the leg and were braced up to the waist-belt by arming-laces at the top. Next the knight put on a tightly fitting

119

pair of mail pants. The body-armour was then put on and buckled over the shoulders and then down the right side. The armour of the arms was next put on and laced to the aketon. His shoulder defences would be put on over the arms, buckled round the upper part of the arm, and laced to the aketon near the neck. Lastly, his gilt spurs would be buckled on over the plate shoes (unless he intended to fight on foot), and his sword and dagger attached with their belt. The gauntlets, buttoned together, would be hung over the sword hilt until required.

The padded arming-cap was now only worn under the helm in the mounted duel with blunt lances. The headpiece would be put on at the last moment. If it was a helm or a basinet with gorget plates, it would be buckled to the breast and back to keep it steady.

Although English brasses and monuments usually show the armour worn without a cover, some monuments and many paint-

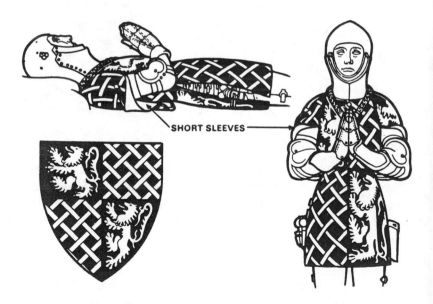

SHORT SLEEVES

The coat of arms of John Fitzalan, Lord Maltravers and Earl of Arundel; about 1435

ings indicate that a variety of jackets was still worn. Some of these were similar to civilian fashions and had long sleeves, and this type was not usually heraldic. Others were the same shape as the modern herald's tabard, open down the sides and with short sleeves covering only the shoulders. This type was usually embroidered or painted with the owner's arms.

Lighter armed cavalry were found along the Scottish border and in Ireland but seem to have been very little used in the French wars. Except that they were usually armed with a light lance and carried a shield, which the heavy cavalry had given up, they were dressed like the infantry.

The armour of the foot soldiers must have varied enormously, depending on the wealth of their village or town, or of their captain, and on what armour they captured or could afford to buy.

Quilted aketons, very often with long sleeves and deep skirts, were popular at the beginning of the century, usually worn with an open-faced basinet and without leg armour. Later the 'brigandine', a tunic made like a pair of plates but with many small plates of steel or horn riveted to a fabric cover, were very commonly worn instead of an aketon. They sometimes had shoulder defences or even full sleeves made in the same way. Alternatively, the sleeves were of mail or, if the man was very lucky, of plate. Sometimes the stomach or the whole breast of the brigandine was covered by a single steel plate without a fabric cover. The hips were often protected by a mail skirt or mail pants. The few surviving breastplates meant for retainers are intended to be worn without a backplate and would have been held on by straps over the shoulders, crossing on the back like a pair of braces.

Archers are rarely illustrated with more leg armour than a knee defence strapped over their hose, but the better equipped infantry are often shown with complete leg-harness. These, presumably, were mounted infantry rather than marching foot.

At Agincourt, an eye-witness describes the English archers wearing helmets of hardened leather or basketwork reinforced with iron bars, but otherwise without armour except for a quilted doublet. Latterly, the visored salet, the kettle-hat, and an open-

English crossbowman and archer, late 15th century and
(*centre*) infantry man early 15th century. The archer
is wearing a brigandine

faced helmet, not unlike a round-topped basinet without visor or
tippet, were all worn, sometimes over a hood of leather or mail.

Much of the armour of the infantry was probably improvised.
Quite a number of pieces of armour survive which have been
adapted for reuse by a later owner. A painting by an Italian artist
shows a crossbowman wearing a fine cavalry cuirass with the
attachment for a lance-rest, probably booty from an earlier battlefield.

Neither archers nor billmen could use large shields but they
often carried small round shields, called 'bucklers', hung on their
sword hilts or on the belt. These they used at arm's length to
parry blows when they were fighting with their swords. Chaucer's
Yeoman and Miller both carried sword and buckler on their
pilgrimage.

Bucklers

The great rectangular shield, called a 'pavise', held up by a prop at the back, was used to give cover to crossbowmen, archers, and handgunners taking part in sieges.

FIFTEENTH-CENTURY ARMS

The dual-purpose, cut-and-thrust sword continued to be popular, presumably because of its usefulness in cutting down light cavalry and poorly armoured infantry. The blades were similar to those of the fourteenth century but, in order to lighten them without losing any of the stiffness necessary for thrusting, they often had hollow-ground edges giving them a cross-section as in figure A. Alternatively, they were made with parallel faces with a high rib running up the centre of each which gave the blades a cross-section as in figure B. The blades vary from very broad and rather short (28 in.) fitted with single-handed hilts, to rather narrow and long (40 in.) fitted with long hilts for occasional use with both hands. Pommels were either wheel-shaped, or pear- or kite-shaped, or of some other elongated form. The cross-guards, which tended to be rather longer than before, were straight, or curved towards the blade, or

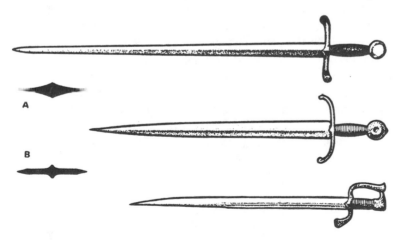

Fifteenth-century swords. The lowest one is single-edged and has a knuckle-guard

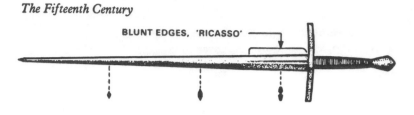

BLUNT EDGES, 'RICASSO'

Fifteenth-century thrusting sword

very occasionally slightly S-shaped.

Purely thrusting swords continued to be used, normally with rather long narrow blades of diamond cross-section, and with long hilts to balance the weight of the blade. Occasionally, the first six inches in front of the cross-guard were made blunt so that the blade could be gripped there by the left hand when it was necessary to use the sword at very close quarters.

From the middle of the century the English infantry began to carry short single-edged swords with the front part of the cross-guard bent up parallel to the grip so as to give protection to the knuckles.

On the Continent a number of additional guards were being developed. A loop was added to protect the forefinger where it passed over the front cross-guard; this was later balanced by a second loop on the rear cross-guard. These two loops were later called the arms of the hilt. As time went on the outer ends of these loops were joined together by a third loop. Some swords had a ring on the side of the cross-guard sticking out at right angles to the axis of the blade. By the end of the century many Continental swords had a combination of these guards, usually with a knuckle guard as well, but these types of hilt do not seem to have been popular in England before the sixteenth century.

The sword was at first still hung on the hip-belt which was sometimes fixed permanently to the skirt of the armour and hinged open with it, but during the first half of the century there was a return to the diagonal belt, now attached by small rings to the metal mount at the top of the scabbard. In the second half of the century that part of the diagonal belt which passed round the back was divided to form a Y shape. The lower arm of the belt was now attached to the scabbard about a foot below the top which made it hang with the point a little to the rear, thus preventing the owner from tripping over it. German and Flemish illustrations occasionally show the scabbard tied down to the thigh in precisely the way that gunmen in the American West tied down their holsters. Normally, to draw his sword the knight had to hold his scabbard down with the left hand; tying it down saved him having to do this.

The scabbard was often fitted with pockets near the top in which a small eating knife and a bodkin or a steel for sharpening the blade could be carried.

Although there were a number of different types of daggers in use in the fifteenth century, the one usually carried by the knightly classes was the rondel dagger. It had a disc-shaped guard in front of the hand and either a conical pommel or a disc-shaped one set on to the grip like a wheel on its axle. The blade was usually triangular in cross-section but more suitable for stabbing than cutting. The infantry, no doubt, all carried a knife or dagger of some sort, partly for eating and partly for dispatching those unable to pay a goodly ransom.

The weapons found most suitable for fighting on foot, in the field or in the barriers, were four- to six-foot-shafted axes with a heavy beak or a hammer head on the back of the head. Narrow strips of steel were nailed down each side of the shaft to prevent the head from being chopped off in action. The shaft had a stout and very sharp spike at each end and a circular steel guard was fitted in front of the hand. This weapon, called a 'ravensbill' or a 'pol-axe', was sufficiently heavy to break into even the strongest armour.

Rondel dagger, about 1490

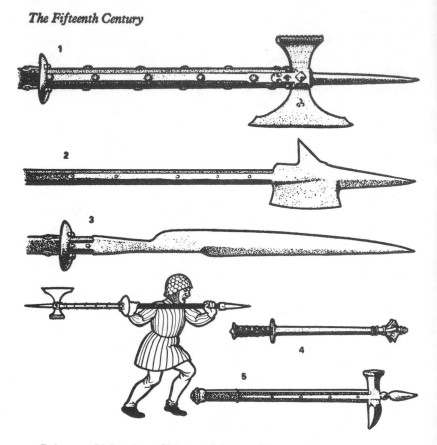

1. Polaxe. 2. Halberd. 3. Glaive. 4. Mace. 5. Horseman's hammer

It is said that the skulls of a number of knights, killed with the very similar Swiss halberd, have been excavated and show that they really were split down to the teeth.

The 'glaive', a stout one-edged blade on a long staff, suitable for both cutting and thrusting, and again fitted with a circular hand-guard, was also popular and so was the *Ahlspeiss*, simply a long steel spike of square cross-section useful for thrusting into the joints of an armour. From their formation in the middle of the fifteenth century, the glaive was the characteristic weapon of the

126

Scots Guard of the Kings of France. Some of the archers, in addition to their sword, also carried mallets and axes with which they speedily dispatched the French knights at Agincourt. The bill remained a popular infantry weapon for those not trained as archers.

The halberd was a cleaver-like axe with a stout spike on the top and a spike or hook on the back of the head. It was attached to the shaft by long steel tongues riveted to the sides of the wood to prevent the head from being cut off and to strengthen the top of the staff.

The lance of the heavy cavalry was now made fatter before and behind the hand, tapering towards each end, and was almost always fitted with a large circular guard in front of the hand; the light cavalry carried a plain shaft. The pike, a very long infantry spear, was popularized by the Swiss armies and was adopted by all their adversaries towards the end of the century. England, immersed in her internal wars, failed to adopt this weapon or the tactics required to make use of it, and the pike only reached this country during the military reforms of Henry VIII's reign.

TOURNAMENTS IN THE FIFTEENTH CENTURY

On the Continent many different kinds of tournament were devised, often requiring special forms of armour. In England, however, probably because of the expense of these special armours, only three mounted combats were popular.

Two of these were duels between riders armed with lances only and, after the 1420's, a wooden barrier, called the 'tilt', was placed between the contestants to prevent their horses from colliding. The horsemen rode along opposite sides of the tilt with their shield sides towards it and pointed their lances across the tilt at their opponent.

For one of these duels, the 'joust of peace', lances with three-pronged heads were used so that they could not pierce the plates. This joust seems to have been looked on as something recalling 'the good old days', the golden age of chivalry. The armour used,

A 'Joust of peace' in the late 15th century. In this case the body-armour is of plate not brigandine

the great helm and the shield, both long outmoded for war, and a body often of brigandine, show that there was a harking back to the past. In fact, the great helm had developed considerably from the fourteenth-century type. The upper edge of the face-plate jutted out below the sight and the skull-plate was much flatter than formerly, giving the helm rather a frog-faced look. At first the helm was strapped down to the body at the front and the back. Later, when the steel cuirass replaced the brigandine, the helm was bolted to it. Shortly after the middle of the century English jousting helms were often made so that the front part could be taken off and replaced by a gorget plate and a visor to make a basinet for foot-combat. A special heavy lance-rest was used for the joust of peace. Secured by staples in the Italian fashion, it was hollow and was filled with a block of wood. The ring behind the handgrip of the lance was fitted with spikes which dug into the wood to give a firm grip.

The second duel, the 'joust of war', was run with sharp lances, but latterly these were not usually as sharp as fighting lances. In this case the normal field-armour (armour for battle) was worn, usually with an armet and wrapper, and, by the middle of the century, with a large reinforce for the left elbow and another, called a 'grandguard' on the left shoulder.

The third type of duel, the course 'at large' or 'at random', was identical to the last but was run without a barrier and, once the lances had been broken or dropped, the duellers removed the cumbersome reinforces from the left arm and set about one another with blunt swords. Often more than one pair of knights took part at the same time and it was this that people of the day called 'the tournament'.

A special form of the tournament, fought with clubs and blunt swords, was popular on the Continent and is shown in one English illustration. The body-armour was a brigandine, and the head-piece a great basinet with a grille-like visor to combine the maximum ventilation with the maximum protection.

The armour for the foot-combat in the barriers was the normal field-armour, and the precise choice of what to wear was left to the contestants. The English seem to have preferred particularly a heavy basinet with a rounded visor, the whole thing buckled or bolted to the cuirass. The usual weapons were casting-spear, pol-axe, sword, and dagger. A shield was carried but was normally hurled at one's opponent before taking to the axe. Usually the number of blows with each weapon was limited, and they had to be delivered by each contestant in turn. Occasionally the challenge states that the fight is to continue until one or other is knocked down. English challenges sometimes include archery contests, wrestling, and casting the bar.

As chivalry gradually became more artificial and divorced from everyday life, the tournament turned into a glamourised form of display. Although the fighting itself became only a little less dangerous, it was now wrapped up in much ceremonious make-believe.

Weddings, treaties, and royal visits were all excuses for extravagant pageantry of which tournaments formed part. In the fourteenth century the 'challenge' was usually a straightforward defiance sent by one group of knights to another or to the world in general. By the end of the fifteenth century the world of make-believe was dominant. The challenge was often very elaborate and was based on a mythical story, like the Tournament of the Shepherdess when the heroine of the joust, Jeanne de Laval, the beloved of King René of Anjou, was dressed as a shepherdess in a thatched cottage guarding her sheep, and her knights were disguised as shepherds. English tournaments were not usually as elaborate as the great Continental ones.

The rules of the tournament and the type of combats were proclaimed by heralds throughout the realm and even at foreign courts. At the place appointed, the lists would be laid out and the ground sanded. A grandstand would be built for the judges, the ladies and gentlemen of the court, and the musicians; it would be decorated with flowers, tapestry, and flags. Tents would be set up in which the contestants could arm themselves. At one end of the lists some tall object, such as a tree, a lily, or a unicorn, would be erected, and on this would be hung the different coloured shields, each representing a different combat. On the appointed day those who accepted the challenge, the Comers, touched the shields representing the different combats in which they wished to take part, and the heralds would then record their names and arms. The Defenders would take it in turns to meet one of the Comers. During the fight, trumpeters and drummers played and cannon were fired. The judge was helped in keeping the score by heralds and pursuivants, and, if he thought that the fight was becoming too dangerous, he could throw down his baton or arrow, the badge of his authority, and order the guards of the Constable or Marshal of the lists to separate the contestants.

All the combats of one kind might take place on one day or during one week, or they might be fought alternately with the other combats of the challenge. In a few cases tournaments lasted for a whole year, although fighting only took place on one or two days of each month and only the Defenders would be there all the time.

Sometimes, on the last day of the tournament, a special combat was held in which all those who had already taken part fought again. This was a mounted contest between two teams or the assault on foot of an imitation castle. Finally, there was a great banquet with many elaborate courses with Interludes acted between them. The prizes were then awarded, usually jewels or weapons either of gold or at least gilt.

The knight-errant still existed in this period; some were genuinely trying to copy the knights of King Arthur's Round Table, others made a good thing out of going from tournament to tournament in order to win rich prizes and the horses and armours of those they defeated. Many of these were professional bullies and were recognised as such; the kings of the realms they visited gave orders that their challenges were not to be accepted.

Often confused with the tournament, but really quite different, was the Trial by Combat. This was a method of trial based on the idea that God would not let the guilty man win. For instance, if a man of gentle birth were accused of murder or treason, he could challenge his accuser to a fight to the death in front of the King sitting as the supreme judge of the realm. The fight was regulated by very strict rules so as to give neither side an advantage. The King sometimes provided the armour and arms, and the arena was prepared on his orders. The fight was to the finish or until the King stopped it and gave judgement. If the accused man lost and was not already dead, he was dragged from the arena and executed. Probably the best-known case is the trial between the Dukes of Norfolk and Hereford in 1398, in front of Richard II, when the King stopped the fight and gave judgement, but as late as 1817 a man accused of murder challenged his accuser to mortal combat by throwing down a gauntlet in the court. He was acquitted because, not surprisingly, his accuser refused the challenge. For those not of gentle birth, the combat was held in front of one of the Royal Judges, the weapon a club or a pick, and the only armour a shield.

FIFTEENTH-CENTURY TACTICS

The motives of Henry V in attacking France were probably as much the need to keep his barons occupied and to establish his dynasty by the glory of a successful war as a genuine belief in the claim to the throne of France. The nobles of France were at each other's throats over which faction should govern during the insanity of the King: the followers of John the Fearless, Duke of Burgundy, or the party of the murdered Louis, Duke of Orleans, brother of the mad King. It was an ideal moment for Henry to lay claim to the formerly English provinces of France.

The invasion of France in 1415 was particularly carefully organised, and the army was accompanied by surgeons, a large train of artillery and supplies, a corps of caterers, and a vast number of craftsmen. The teeth of the invasion fleet consisted of some 2,000 men-at-arms, 8,000 archers, and 65 gunners. The destination of the fleet was kept secret, and the divided authorities in France failed to make serious preparations to prevent the English landing. Henry's aim appears to have been to recapture his ancestral Duchy of Normandy, and the first act of the war was the capture of Harfleur at the mouth of the Seine, largely by means of an artillery bombardment.

Henry's next decision, to march with his army from his newly captured base 160 miles across northern France to Calais, was possibly due to a wish to imitate his illustrious great-grandfather, Edward III, or to show the world that he could march through the lands he claimed as his own without meeting any resistance. He left his wagons behind and marched as lightly as possible, which suggests that he wished in fact to travel so fast that the French would be unable to catch up with him. In this he was foiled by having to make a long detour to avoid the well-guarded crossings of the flooded Somme.

On 24 October 1415 the English army, hungry and exhausted by the long march and by dysentery, found the French army, vastly superior in numbers, barring their road in front of the little village of Agincourt. On the following morning Henry drew up his army. The English were so few in number that no reserve was possible and they formed up in a single line consisting of three groups of dismounted knights and men-at-arms with the archers between them and on the flanks. The Duke of York, the King's uncle, commanded the right wing, Lord Camoys the left, and the King himself the centre. Apparently warned that the French planned to concentrate their attack on his archers, the King ordered them to plant stout stakes in the ground in front of them, sharpened at the top and pointing forward at the level of a horse's chest. Except for the absence of a reserve, the tactics of the English were unchanged from those of the fourteenth century.

Since they had last fought the English, the French had defeated an army of Flemish infantry at Roosebeke in 1382. Their tactics on that day had been a frontal attack by dismounted men-at-arms, combined with simultaneous flank attacks by cavalry. The combination of pressures had thrust the Flemings into a helpless mass in which many had died from suffocation. These were the tactics the French were to employ at Agincourt, but the English, unlike the Flemings, had their flanks resting on two thick woods and could not be outflanked.

The French commanders, the Constable Charles d'Albret and the Dukes of Orleans and Bourbon, drew up their army, consisting of some 24,000 men, in three divisions. The first was dismounted men-at-arms and knights but had flanks of cavalry, the second was entirely dismounted, while the rear division all remained on horseback.

Neither side was willing to begin the attack, and it was not until eleven o'clock that Henry gave the signal to advance. The English halted as soon as they came within bowshot, replanted their stakes, and began to shoot. The French then began to advance. The cavalry attacks on the archers on the flanks of the army were beaten off, and the retreating horsemen and riderless horses galloping through the front division of the advancing French flung them into disorder. This disorder was increased as the French came on, since they tended to bunch in front of the English men-at-arms, pressing away from the English bowmen. The arrival of the French second line made the chaos worse, and it became impossible to move or wield a weapon. The English archers flung aside their bows and fell to handstrokes with their swords, axes, and mallets. The slaughter was terrible, and one eye-witness declared that more died in the press than were killed by the English. In half an hour the battle was over, a great wall of dead lay in front of the exhausted English line, and a great number of prisoners had been taken. The third French line made no attack; indeed, it probably could not have got over the wall of dead. However, during the gathering up of prisoners and the sorting out of the wounded from the dead, the English baggage-park was attacked by another body of French, and at the same time the enemy's third line appeared to be about to advance. Since they probably outnumbered the English and were fresh, Henry had to act swiftly. No one could be spared to guard the prisoners. The King therefore instantly ordered their execution and many were dispatched before it was discovered that no further attack was going to be made.

The fact that this tiny army could inflict some 10,000 casualties on the French, including three dukes, some ninety lords, and 1,500 knights, as well as capturing the three commanders, gave Henry enormous prestige and made possible all that followed. Like Crécy, it gave the English the ascendancy of morale over the French. By 1419 the whole of Normandy was in English hands, and the rival French factions decided to make up their quarrel in the face of the common foe. At the peace conference the Duke of Burgundy was murdered by the Orleans party; his heir immediately joined forces with the English, the Queen of France gave her daughter as wife to Henry v and repudiated her own son. By the Treaty of Troyes (1420) Henry was appointed regent of France and heir to the throne. With Burgundy as an ally and a general like Henry in command, France might indeed one day be conquered.

Two years later Henry was dead and in his place his brother, the Duke of Bedford, was regent for the baby Henry vi of England and ii of France. Bedford was a good general and a better diplomat. In spite of a chronic shortage of troops, many of whom were required for garrisons, he won notable victories at Cravant in 1423 and Verneuil in 1424, and he slowly consolidated and extended the English conquests. He strengthened the Burgundian alliance. His task was made more difficult by quarrels in the Council at home, and the falling away of his allies, beginning with Brittany. In 1428 Bedford received reinforcements and began the siege of Orleans, the last important stronghold in French hands north of the River Loire. The difference in morale of the two nations is clear; the heavily defended city was on the point of surrendering to a very inferior force of besiegers, when events took an amazing turn.

The story of the relief of Orleans by Joan of Arc is too well known to need repeating here. Her effect on French morale was instantaneous and she gave her compatriots the dash which had previously been the monopoly of the English. Her success in the field was probably due to her enthusiasm, which led her to attack the English before they took up their usual impregnable, defensive position. The loyalty of the French in the conquered areas was aroused, and the crowning of the young Charles VII at Rheims gave them hope for a revival of French power.

Finally, growing enmity between the English and the Burgundians led to the break-up of the alliance in 1435. The Duke of Burgundy allied himself with the French King by the Treaty of Arras, and a week later Bedford died. If France could not be conquered with the aid of Burgundy, it certainly could not be conquered with Burgundy on the other side. Castles held by Burgundian forces became enemies overnight. The English were able to hold on because of that stubbornness which prevents them from knowing when the game is lost. The Burgundians soon made peace, since so much of their wealth depended on the English wool trade. France was not only still too exhausted to fight properly but was being ravaged by bands of her own unpaid mercenaries. Even after the Treaty of Arras the English could still beat the French in the open field, and a writer of the time could say: 'Whenever the French find themselves with a superiority of three to one they at once retreat.'

135

The occupied areas of France were too impoverished to pay for the war. The English parliament was unwilling to vote the huge sums necessary to pay sufficient garrisons and to maintain castles, and although the people of England were eager for more victories they were unwilling to pay taxes to hire the necessary troops. The Council was distracted by the quarrels of those, like Cardinal Beaufort, who wanted to make peace, and those, like Gloucester, who thought that to make peace was to surrender and who were incapable of admitting that Henry v had been wrong. Few saw that ultimate victory was impossible.

In the meantime, a great military reorganisation was taking place in France. Firstly, the Treasurer of the French Royal Household, Jacques Cœur, put the Royal finances on a stable basis. Secondly, the Constable Richemont and the Count de Dunois organised the standing army set up by the Ordinances of 1439 and 1448. These were intended to put the marauding bands of mercenaries on a regular footing and to prevent private wars between barons. In future only the King might raise companies, and all captains were to be chosen by him. The troops were to be regularly paid from a special tax formerly levied by the barons and now only to be levied by the King. Pillage was forbidden, and companies were subject to the normal law of the land. By 1445 fifteen companies of these *gens d'ordonnance* had been raised, each consisting of one hundred men-at-arms, each with a page, two archers, and a light-armed soldier, all mounted. The Ordinance of 1448 stated that each village must equip and pay for one archer. In time of war they would receive wages from the Crown. A little later regulations were made about the arming and armour of these village archers (*franc archiers*).

Finally, the Royal artillery was reorganised by the brothers Bureau, and their efficiency can be gauged by the swiftness with which the English-held castles, admittedly undermanned and in disrepair, fell in the lightning campaign of 1449.

The last battle of the Hundred Years War, Castillon in Gascony, was totally different from any of the earlier ones. On this occasion it was the French who had taken up a prepared position, in this case a fortified camp with a ditch, rampart, and a palisade lined with many guns apparently placed so as to give crossfire. The English under one of their most famous captains, John Talbot, Earl of Shrewsbury, were forced, because of the lie of the ground, to make a frontal attack. They did not wait for the arrival of their archers, who might have cleared the palisade, and were in consequence crushingly defeated and their commander killed.

The battles of the Wars of the Roses were fought in the typical English formation of groups of dismounted men-at-arms flanked by archers. The shower of arrows at the opening of the battle was usually too fierce to bear and both sides hurriedly closed in for the hand-to-hand fighting. Only at Northampton did the Yorkists build a palisaded camp like that at Castillon, but heavy rain made their guns useless. The only leader who comes out of these wars with any military distinction is Edward IV, who was never defeated in the field and was a master of the well-timed march, regularly outmanœuvring his opponents, as on the Tewkesbury campaign of 1471.

CASTLES AND CANNONS IN THE FIFTEENTH CENTURY

The castles built in the fifteenth century were either lightly fortified manor houses or stately palaces with defences more for the sake of prestige than for use. Fortifications of a new type were built but these were not residences and are therefore forts rather than true castles. They were intended to be defended by gunfire and were strategically placed to protect harbours. The Corporation of Dartmouth built a small gun-fort with square gun-embrasures covering the entrance to their haven in about 1480. In Scotland an ambitious coastal-defence scheme was planned for the Firth of Forth to protect the sea approaches to Edinburgh and the central Lowlands. The only part of this actually completed was the castle of Ravenscraig in Fife, the main defence of which was its guns.

English artillery helped to capture Harfleur in 1415 and battered down the walls of Le Mans within a few days in 1424. Many

Dartmouth Fort from the sea; about 1480

of the English garrisons surrendered on the appearance of the French siege-train in the great campaign of reconquest of 1449. The development of the gun was temporarily ahead of improvements in fortifications.

Sieges were conducted in exactly the same way as before, with guns replacing engines, but instead of the mines being filled with inflammable material they were filled with gunpowder. So that the force of the explosion should not blow back on the besiegers down the straight tunnel, the mine was dug with several sharp corners in the passage.

The largest guns were still fired lying on the ground from behind a pivoted shutter which gave cover to the crew while working the gun, but could be swung up out of the way at the moment of firing. Many other guns were now much more mobile and were mounted on wheeled carriages on which they could actually be fired as well as transported. Sometimes several small guns were mounted on one cart. Breech-loaders were very common. The breech-block was shaped rather like a beer mug, with a handle for lifting it in and out of the gun, and was pierced near the back by a touch-hole. It was filled with powder, the ball was placed in the

138

Fifteenth-century gun emplacement with shutter

barrel, and the breech-block put in behind it and wedged tight in a frame made in one with the gun barrel.

At first, guns were merely held on to the carts by iron straps. By about 1470 guns were being made with a small cylindrical block sticking out at each side a little in front of the point of balance. These blocks, called 'trunnions', rested in hollows on the side of the carriage and acted as pivots allowing the muzzle of the gun to be raised and lowered to increase or decrease the range. The

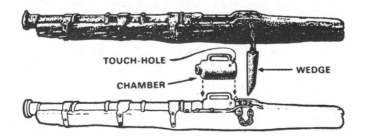

Mid fifteenth-century light cannon

139

Late fifteenth-century light cannon with elevating quadrant

movement of the muzzle was regulated on the smaller guns by fitting the breech end into a quadrant, and on the larger ones by pushing in or pulling out a large wooden wedge under the breech end. The carriages had iron-shod wheels to strengthen them against the battering of rough roads. The siege-train of guns and ammunition wagons, drawn by large numbers of horses or oxen, was accompanied by many pioneers to level roads and right over-turned guns. As well as gunners in the regular pay of the Crown, blacksmiths and others would be called up to man the guns in time of war.

Iron guns were made on the hoop-and-stave principle already described, and two of these left behind by the English at Mont St Michel in 1423 are respectively 12 foot and 11 foot 9 inches long with calibres (i.e. internal diameters) of 18 inches and 15 inches. A similar gun at Edinburgh called 'Mons Meg', which was probably made in Flanders before 1460, is 13 foot 2 inches long with a calibre of 19½ inches and fires a stone ball weighing 549 pounds. One ball from this gun is said to have been retrieved from a distance of two miles. Guns as large as this were fired lying on the ground, and 'Mons' was accompanied on campaign by a crane to lift it on and off its travelling carts. Gunners gave these large guns pet names like 'Foul mouthed Meg', another Scots gun,

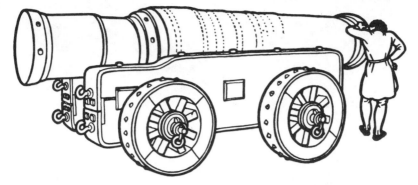

'Mons Meg' on her reconstructed travelling carriage (Edinburgh Castle)

and each size of smaller gun had a name – falcons, sakers (i.e. sparrow hawks) culverins (i.e. snakes) and basiliskes. These names indicate only very vaguely the size of the guns since there was no uniformity of barrel-length or calibre.

Large guns were also being cast in brass. One, now at Basle in Switzerland, was captured from the Burgundians at Granson in 1476. Similar guns, but covered with highly moulded decoration, were apparently being cast in Italy. By 1474 James III of Scotland had a gun foundry in Edinburgh Castle casting bronze guns. Masons were employed to cut gun-stones, which were preferred, because, being lighter than iron, they could be fired with a smaller charge of powder, and the gun was therefore less likely to burst. James II of Scotland was killed by a bursting cannon at the siege of Roxburgh in 1460.

Great care had to be taken to swab out these big guns with a long wet mop before reloading them, in case any red-hot ashes remained inside. The new charge was put in by means of a very long-handled ladle and compressed with a rammer. The ball was rolled in and pushed tightly home.

On long journeys gunpowder was often shaken so badly that the ingredients tended to settle out at different levels in the barrels, sulphur at the bottom, carbon at the top, and saltpetre in the

141

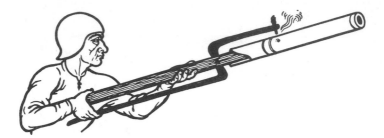

Early fifteenth-century gun lock

middle. Before going into action it all had to be remixed. Before the end of the fifteenth century corned-powder was discovered. This did not settle out, and was less affected by damp in the air. It was made by moistening gunpowder with a mixture of alcohol and water, drying it out, and then breaking the cake which resulted into tiny crumbs, each of which would contain some of the three ingredients stuck firmly together. Unfortunately it was found to explode too fiercely for the old-fashioned hoop-and-stave guns and could only be used in the relatively stronger handguns and cast brass guns.

The handguns (ancestors of muskets and rifles) of the early fifteenth century were small cannons either simply lashed to a wooden stock or made with a socket for the wooden shaft. They were aimed by placing the stock or shaft either under the arm or over the shoulder and were fired by a piece of wire red-hot at the end, or by a piece of burning slow-match held in the hand. Occasionally this was done by an assistant, which allowed the gunner a firmer grip for his aim. 'Slow-match' was a slowly burning cord made of hemp or flax tow soaked in saltpetre and then dried out. Sometimes the shaft was long enough to stick into the ground when the gun was being fired. As the century progressed the barrel was lengthened and was almost always of the type lashed to the stock; the rear part of the stock was bent down slightly so as to

142

rest against the chest, the touch-hole was moved to the right side of the barrel and provided with a movable cover, and the burning slow-match was held mechanically. The earliest form of gun lock consisted of a Z-shaped lever, called the 'serpentine', pivoting on the side of the stock. The short upper arm of the lever held the match over the pan. By pressing up the long rear arm, which lay parallel to the stock, the burning match was pushed down into the pan. Later fifteenth-century guns were fitted with a more developed variety of lock, in which the rear lever and the match-holder were made separately but were connected by a spring-loaded lever. Pressure on the rear lever lowered the match-holder gently into the pan against the action of the spring. This prevented the match accidentally swinging into the pan when the gunner was not ready. The figure shows a later development. The works of this sort of lock were let into the side of the stock and covered by a metal plate to protect them from damage. This type of lock remained in use until about 1600.

Many early handguns were fitted with a stout lug underneath which could be hooked over a parapet to take the kick of the explosion. This continued to be used on the larger wall-guns and

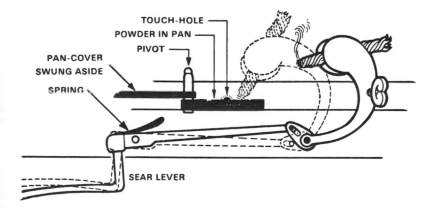

The spring-loaded matchlock mechanism

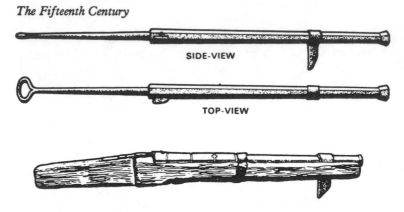

SIDE-VIEW

TOP-VIEW

Fifteenth-century handguns

those fired in battle from a trestle until the sixteenth century. In England this type was called a 'hackbut' or 'arquebus' but by the middle of the sixteenth century these names were used for the ordinary infantry handgun. By the seventeenth century 'arquebus' referred only to a cavalry handgun.

Handguns were now accurate enough to be used for shooting game but this did not become popular until the following century.

Chapter Seven

The First Half of the Sixteenth Century

HENRY VIII's REORGANISATION

The Wars of the Roses virtually extinguished the old feudal aristo-cracy. 'Livery and Maintenance' was stamped out by heavy fines against offenders. Thus England was left without an effective army. At the beginning of the reign of Henry VIII (1509–47) the only regular troops in the kingdom were the Yeomen of the Guard, the gunners of the various castles, and the small garrison of Calais. Most other monarchs had by now some form of standing army.

Henry added to the Yeomen of the Guard a second body, 'the King's Spears'. This consisted of fifty gentlemen who served in full armour and on armoured horses. Each had a mounted archer, a light-armed horseman, carrying a light lance or boar-spear, and a servant. This Guard was present at the Battle of Guinegate in 1513. For the time being they proved too expensive but were re-organised in about 1539 and survive today as the Queen's Body-guard, the Gentlemen-at-Arms, who bear on their standard 'Guinegate', the oldest battle honour of the British Army. When on palace duty and in attendance on foot they carried gilt pol-axes but wore civilian clothes in some uniform colours which appear to have changed from time to time. They were used both as a bodyguard and as a corps of trained officers to command troops in the absence of the King.

Henry, like most of his contemporaries, wished to win personal military glory by conquests. His prowess in the tiltyard was legendary but the forces at his command made it difficult to repeat these victories in the field. His lack of a regular army was made more unfortunate by new developments in warfare on the Continent. The many victories of the Swiss with their massive columns of pikemen had made this the major infantry weapon of all European armies. Improved handguns had replaced both the longbow and crossbow as missile support weapons, and heavy cavalry had come back into their own. Both the French and German armies contained large organised bodies of men-at-arms mounted on armoured horses.

The English infantry were still almost entirely archers and billmen as was seen on the Flodden campaign of 1513. Although they defeated the Scots, who were newly trained in the continental pike tactics but unsupported by missile weapons, they could not compete with the heavy cavalry, pikemen, and handgunners of foreign armies.

There was a shortage of heavy horses in England and only the King's Spears and some of the greatest nobles were able to serve on armoured horses. Many gentlemen served as light cavalry, called demilances, or on foot. Mounted archers accompanied the cavalry at Guinegate but they dismounted and shot at the flanks of the French cavalry from behind the cover of some hedges.

The wealth amassed by his father allowed Henry to hire foreign mercenaries of the types he needed, and in the large numbers he required. The pikemen and heavy cavalry were usually Burgundians or Germans, and his handgunners Spaniards or Italians. Even at the end of his reign, after all his efforts at military reform, he still required many thousands of foreign mercenaries for the 'Enterprise of Boulogne' of 1544.

Henry VII had continued to use the contract system for his foreign campaigns. His son seems to have given up the contract itself, but his expeditionary forces still largely consisted of men raised by the gentry and nobles from among their household servants, tenants, and dependants. Tenants were obliged by the ancient customs of the manor to fight for their lords, although they could probably get off by providing substitutes. The gentry were assessed according to the property they owned, and had to provide a proportionate number of men which might vary between two from a small squire and many hundred from a great noble. The tenants and dependants of abbeys, bishoprics, colleges, and Royal manors would have to follow the steward of the estate, who might in fact be a noble with a large following of his own. In the north of England, where the danger of a Scottish invasion was always present, many farms were let for mixed rents of money and military service. Age, youth, or sickness might keep a landowner from serving himself, or he might already hold a government post or be a clergyman, so he would be ordered to send his men alone; others would be ordered to serve in person as captains. Officers were supposed to be chosen for their experience of warfare but Thomas Audley, writing at the time, said that English officers were more often chosen by favouritism.

As before, the militia continued to exist alongside this semi-feudal organisation and in this period was largely used for home defence. Henry VIII saw that it required strengthening. In 1511 he reissued the old Statute of Winchester of 1285 to remind everyone of the weapons, armour, and horses each class must possess. The Commissioners of Array were ordered to muster the militia and find out whether the statute was being obeyed. The wealth of those inadequately armed was to be calculated, and they were to be ordered to buy the arms suitable for their rank. If they failed to do so they were to be fined. In 1522 Henry held a new 'Domesday' survey to record the wealth of every man in each county and to make a list of the arms which he possessed. The result showed that few had the necessary arms and that hardly any parishes had armour for their men. More muster parades were ordered until the position improved. Acts were passed for the encouragement of archery and the building of shooting butts on every village green where everyone was to practise on holidays. Every man between sixteen and sixty years of age must possess a bow and know how to use it.

The Commissioners of Array seem usually to have been the Justices of the Peace, possibly because the Statute of Winchester was originally designed for keeping the peace. Towards the end

147

of the reign these Commissioners were usually placed under a lieutenant appointed by the King, who supervised their activities. It was he who now received the commission to raise the forces required and to appoint the Commissioners of Array. Together they divided the number of men required by the government between the hundreds[1] of each shire, called out the full militia, and then chose the most suitable men. In theory only sickness exempted a man from service, but in fact the gentry were immune except for service as officers. The Commissioners were expected to choose able-bodied men, if possible experienced in war, the unemployed, and local trouble-makers.

The King tried to increase the number of horses in the kingdom by an act laying down the number to be kept by every rank of society from a duke or archbishop with seven, down to a commoner with an annual income of £100 who had to have one horse. Any man whose wife wore a velvet skirt or a silk petticoat had to keep a horse regardless of his income.

HENRY VIII's REFORMS

Far, far more important than Henry's continental wars was his reforming work at home. *Firstly*, he laid the foundations of the Royal Navy, adding the naval dockyards at Deptford and Woolwich to the one set up by his father at Portsmouth, encouraging the design of larger and faster ships, and keeping up a permanent establishment of ships, men, and administration. The new ships were floating gun-batteries, intended to fight gun duels and avoid closing with enemy ships and boarding. The Royal Navy and Elizabethan encouragement of overseas ventures made possible competition with Spain in the planting of colonies in the New World.

Secondly, from 1539 Henry fortified the coast from Hull round to Milford Haven with a series of artillery forts of a new pattern. His fleet was dependent on the wind and might not be able to put to sea at a moment when invasion threatened. Hitherto raiders had had to land to do any damage; now they could stand offshore and bombard coastal towns and shipping at anchor in havens.

148

[1] Hundred: the old Saxon administrative area.

The answer was a series of low forts, forming poor targets for guns fired from the moving deck of a ship and difficult to damage because of their immensely thick walls and absence of height. The fort formed a steady platform for a large number of heavy guns to fire at ships, ill-protected by their wooden walls and clearly visible as targets. The plan of these forts is usually circular, with three, four, or six great protruding semicircular bastions carrying guns on the roof and in a lower gallery. Usually there is a low central tower carrying a third tier of guns. Most of them are or were surrounded by a deep dry moat to keep the attackers at a convenient distance. If the enemy got into the moat the defenders could fire on them through the many small handgun openings provided at this level. Living space was always cramped, allowing for a master-gunner and a small regular garrison. In an emergency militia could be sent to augment the permanent staff. The destruction of the newly dissolved monasteries provided much excellent stonework for these structures.

The main forts were placed in the Thames, guarding the approaches to London, and along the south coast, guarding the harbours and anchorages where invasion was most likely, in the Isle of Wight, in the Solent, at Deal, Walmer and Sandgate, and at Falmouth, where each side of the anchorage has its fort, St Mawes and Pendennis.

Left. Walmer Castle, about 1540. *Right.* St. Mawes Castle, about 1543

149

10 Thirdly, Henry reorganised the national armoury in the Tower of London. The King seems to have emptied the Tower of all old equipment and completely restocked it with vast quantities of up-to-date weapons. An inventory of the Royal Armouries of the Tower, Greenwich, and Westminster made at his death includes 20,100 pikes, 6,700 bills, 7,700 handguns, 3,060 bows, 13,050 sheaves, each of twenty-four arrows, 160 gross of bowstrings, as well as many other weapons. In 1512 he bought 2,000 light armours from Florence, each costing eleven shillings and each consisting of a salet, a gorget, a breastplate, a backplate, and a pair of light arms. In 1513 he bought 5,000 similar armours from Milan. Under the threat of French invasion in 1539 the King purchased 1,200 complete armours from Cologne and 2,700 from Antwerp, both great centres of the manufacture of munition armour – that is, armour for the ordinary soldier.

0 Although he was a great archer himself, able to beat the bowmen of his own guard chosen from the best archers in the kingdom, and encouraged the practice of archery by statute and proclamation, the King clearly saw the importance of hand firearms. He always hired foreign handgunners, both infantry and cavalry, for his campaigns, and he authorised the use of handguns as well as bows in the village butts. Even in the early years of his reign he was purchasing hundreds of handguns overseas. He had several expensive guns of his own and many matchlock guns from Italy, some of them breech-loading. Latterly the mounted portion of the guard was apparently equipped with a shorter gun carried in a holster. Probably on some occasions the guard carried the round, steel shields with a breech-loading matchlock pistol fixed so as to fire through the centre which are still in the Tower of London. Some, perhaps those of the officers, were decorated with etching and gilding. By the end of the reign the Royal Armouries at the Tower, Greenwich, and Westminster contained twice as many firearms as bows. The very large numbers of pikes in stock show how hard Henry was working to bring his army up to date. In spite of all these efforts, the muster of the levies in 1539 showed that, although the number of pikemen and handgunners had greatly increased, they were still vastly outnumbered by archers and billmen.

Fourthly, as soon as he came to the throne Henry began his efforts to improve the artillery train begun by his father and all-important in dominating barons contemplating revolt. He appointed a bell founder, Master Humphrey Walker, gunner at the Tower, and set him to work casting guns. He ordered forty-eight guns from Hans Poppenruyter, the Master Founder of Malines in Flanders, one of the most famous makers of the day. A further forty-eight were ordered from him for the Navy in 1512. He attempted to intercept the guns being made in Flanders for the Scots, and robbed the great Venetian trading fleet of guns. Twelve of the guns ordered from Poppenruyter were called 'The Twelve Apostles', and the order stipulated that each should shoot a ball of 20 pounds of iron with a similar weight of powder and must be capable of firing thirty times a day. In the following year the Venetian ambassador reported that Henry had 'cannon enough to conquer hell'.

To avoid having to rely on imported artillery, the King brought over Peter Baude, a Frenchman, and the Arcanus brothers of Cesena in Italy to set up gun foundries respectively at Hounds-ditch and at Salisbury Place near Fleet Street. Baude, as well as casting many guns, trained English gunfounders in the art, including the Owen brothers who succeeded him as the King's gun-founders. A three-barrelled breech-loading gun signed by Baude is in the Tower of London; it is described in a contemporary inventory as 'Brode fawcons shoting iij shotte' (Broad falcons shoot-ing three shots). A gun formerly signed by one of the Arcanus family and dated 1542 and another dated 1546 by the Owen brothers are also in the Tower. Gunpowder mills were set up in the Tower and in Sussex.

At the King's death the Tower Armouries contained 64 brass guns and 351 of iron, of all sizes. Two of these were Venetian, two were French, and seventeen were Scottish, either captured at Flodden and elsewhere or confiscated in Flanders before delivery. The variety of names given to artillery at this period is astonishing

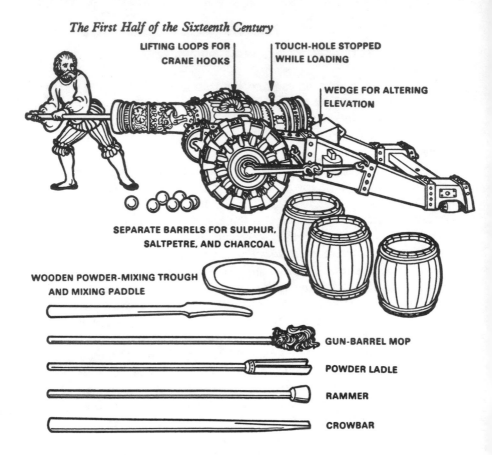

LIFTING LOOPS FOR
CRANE HOOKS

TOUCH-HOLE STOPPED
WHILE LOADING

WEDGE FOR ALTERING
ELEVATION

SEPARATE BARRELS FOR SULPHUR,
SALTPETRE, AND CHARCOAL

WOODEN POWDER-MIXING TROUGH
AND MIXING PADDLE

GUN-BARREL MOP

POWDER LADLE

RAMMER

CROWBAR

Early sixteenth-century artillery

and baffling – basiliskes, cannons, demi-cannons, bastard cannons, cannon periers, culverins, demy culverins, bastard culverins,
sacres, minions, falcons, falconets, robinettes, various types of
bases, slings, and fowlers, to mention only a few. Writers use
different names for the same guns. Bombards fired shot of 260
pounds, the curtald, which weighed about 3,000 pounds, fired a
shot of 60 pounds, the culverin 20 pounds, the lizard 12 pounds,
and the minion 8 pounds. The success of Henry's policy was shown
in the following reign at the battle of Pinkie, where the Scots were

152

defeated largely by a combination of field and naval gunnery.

Fifthly, Henry set up a Royal armour factory to produce fine armours for his own personal use and as gifts to foreign princes. The King was no doubt inspired by the magnificent armours owned by his ally, the Emperor Maximilian I, and by that given to him by the Emperor in 1514, made in the Imperial Armoury at Innsbruck in Tyrol. In 1511 the King had a group of Italian armourers working for him at Greenwich, as well as a group from Brussels, and the latter continued to work for him for some time after 1515 when the German armourers, who were to form the nucleus of the permanent Royal Armoury, arrived. The Germans were also established at Greenwich not far from the palace. Although they were busy working for the King, they were also allowed to make armours for favoured members of the court, who, no doubt, paid richly for the privilege as well as for the armour. Only five armours that were made by this workshop during Henry's lifetime are known. One is a magnificent suit dated 1527, etched and gilt all over with cherubs among foliage and bearing what may be a Tudor badge. Many people think that this was an armour made for the King himself.

In the reigns of Mary and Elizabeth I there was no real need for a Royal Armoury but it was continued in order to supply rich armours for visiting princes and for the court. The Prince of Finland received one, as did the Earls of Pembroke, Leicester (who had three), and Cumberland, among others, as well as many of the court officials such as Sir Henry Lee, Master of the Armouries, who had three. The Armoury continued to produce excellent suits right into the reign of James I, and the suit of his son Henry is in Windsor Castle. Many of these suits survive or are shown in family portraits.

ARMOUR IN THE FIRST HALF OF THE SIXTEENTH CENTURY

This century saw the development of specialist troops, and many handbooks were written describing how each type should be

153

armed:

THE HEAVY CAVALRY in full armour on armoured horses carrying lance and sword.

LIGHTER CAVALRY armed in a three-quarter armour without greaves or plate shoes, carrying a lighter lance and sword, and by the middle of the century short firearms.

VERY LIGHT HORSE from the Northern borders again carrying a light lance and a sword.

HANDGUNNERS and BOWMEN (generally described together as 'the shot'), often not armoured at all or only with a light open-faced helmet and a quilted jack.

PIKEMEN and BILLMEN usually in armour to the knee with full plate arms and sometimes a close-helmet and sometimes an open-faced helmet.

The simple armours shown in English illustrations of the early part of the century resemble those of Flanders and Italy rather than the more robust fluted armours of Germany. The helmet was usually an armet with a wrapper. This was later replaced by a similarly shaped helmet but made with the front part of the neck pivoting at the same points as the visor. The shoulder defences usually consist of a development of No. 3 on page 111 with a high extension outwards of the top edge of the main plate called the 'haute-piece'. This was borrowed from the Italian reinforce and was intended to give protection against an upward blow at the neck. The breast was rather flat with a central vertical keel and was worn with large shield-shaped tassets usually divided horizontally. The legs were similar to those of the last century but the feet were made with very broad toes to match the civilian shoe. This was the sort of armour worn by the knighthood and heavy cavalry. If the knight wanted to take part in the tilt he could modify his basic armour. First, he removed the haute-piece from his left shoulder or put on a shoulder not fitted with one; then he put on a large reinforce covering the left shoulder and probably part of the face and left breast, a reinforce over the left elbow, and probably another over the left gauntlet. He was then fully prepared.

The armour of light horsemen, known as 'demilances' in Eng-

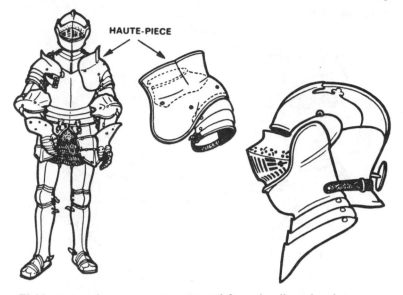

Field-armour about 1514, reconstructed from the silvered and
gilt armour of Henry VIII

land, did not differ from this in form, but the greaves and plate
shoes were replaced by stout leather boots, and instead of a visor
the helmet was often fitted with a peak like a modern cap and a
grille of vertical bars actually over the opening. This type, called
a 'burgonet', could be converted into a sort of close-helmet by
fitting a wrapper over the face. The light cavalry armed with the
short guns, arquebuses about three foot long, that became popular
in the middle of the century, wore armour to the knee, with mail
sleeves and an open-faced helmet. They did not charge home but
rode up near enough to the enemy to fire their pieces and then
rode back to reload.

Many of Henry's light horse drawn from the Border counties
probably only had mail shirts, brigandines, or jacks for body
armour. The 'jack' was the poor man's substitute for the brigandine, with overlapping plates of horn or steel fixed into a canvas
garment quilted with cotton or rags for extra protection and held

155

LEATHER-COVERED 'RICASSO'

German mercenary infantry of about 1530

in place by knotted cords instead of the rivets of the brigandine. One of the surviving ones shows where it has stopped a pistol ball. The English light horse often wore a red cap over their helmet.

The infantry armours imported by Henry from Germany and those of his German mercenary pikemen would be of course in the German fashion, with rounded globose breasts, and long, many-lamed tassets almost reaching to the knee. From this time on armours were made with a collar of narrow horizontal plates, called a 'gorget'. The lower edge was worn under the body-armour. The infantry had by now given up leg armour altogether. Usually the arms were only defended by plates on the outside, while the shoulder defences would cover only the top of the

156

shoulder and the front would be covered by a pointed disc hanging in front of the armpit. The shoulders were sometimes covered by a huge mail tippet. The helmet, often a burgonet, was frequently little more than a skull-cap with a slight lobster-tail neckguard and a peak over the eyes. Many illustrations show only a huge round hat with slashed brim and a large number of gaudy-coloured ostrich feathers. The drummers and fifers of these *Landsknecht* regiments rarely wore any armour at all; nor did the handgunners, who wore the multi-coloured costume. with the white under-garments 'puffed' through many small slits in the doublet and hose, which their exploits in battle made fashionable throughout Europe. The Emperor Charles v, among others, had armours made in steel imitating these puffed and slashed costumes. The officers of these regiments prided themselves on wearing the same fashion of armour as the men but in finer quality, often etched and gilt. Towards the end of Henry's reign the globose breast was replaced by one with a strong vertical keel drawn out to a point just below the centre.

Henry's former Provost Marshal, Thomas Audley, writing about the middle of the century, said: 'I would wish that no shot should have armour upon him but [i.e. except] a morrion or skull upon his head, for there can be no shot, neither archer nor arque-bus, serve well being Armed' [i.e. being armoured]. The 'morion' was a new name for the kettle-hat. Two types were emerging, one with a pointed top called a 'Spanish morion' from its place of origin; the other, which came from Italy, with a raised comb running fore and aft, called a 'comb morion'. In spite of Audley's writings many of the shot had brigandines or jacks. Henry's archers each carried two sharp stakes to stick in the ground in front of their company.

The King himself had a number of special armours made for use only in the tournament and not for the field. One of these for the foot-combat, probably with two-handed swords or sword and shield, has a large bell-shaped, steel skirt. Another, also for the foot-combat, but probably with polaxes, has a completely enclos-ing pair of steel shorts to cover those parts of the top of the legs usually left unguarded because they were covered by the saddle when mounted. The helmet of this armour is made so as to fit tightly round the top of the gorget so that the head could be turned but the helmet could not be knocked off and there was no gap at the neck for a weapon to enter.

By the 1540's, when Henry had a new armour made, he took a leaf out of the old Emperor's book and that of his successor, Charles V. The Emperor Maximilian and his armourer, Lorenz Helmschmied, had devised a way of building an armour with a large number of spare parts and reinforces so that it could be converted for use in many different types of combat and tournament. Henry's new armour was made in this way. Apparently there was a light-horse or pikeman's armour with burgonet, rotating on the gorget, full shoulders without haute-pieces, breast without lance-rest and with laminated tassets to just above the knee. This could be made into a field-armour by the addition of legs, haute-pieces on the shoulders, and a reinforcing breast with lance-rest, and by the replacement of the peak of the burgonet with a field-visor and a wrapper. For the tournament with blunt swords the right gauntlet was replaced by one that locked round the grip of the sword so as to give an unbreakable hold. For the foot-combat a large plate bottom-defence would be buckled in place and the reinforcing breast removed. The tilt-armour differed from the field-armour in being without haute-pieces and wrapper; the helmet has a heavier visor, the left elbow has its usual large reinforce, a special tilting gauntlet with a large cuff was worn over the field gauntlet, and a very large grandguard covered the left shoulder, most of the breast, and the lower part of the visor to which it was bolted in order to prevent the head from being thrust back. In addition to all this there was a second skirt and tassets to give extra defence to the

A reconstruction of Henry VIII's Greenwich garniture of 1540
1. The pikeman's armour, converting into the field-armour 2, which converts into the tilt-armour 3. 4. Gauntlet for the tournament with swords. 5. Bottom-defence for foot-combat.
6. Field-visor and wrapper. 7. Tilt-visor

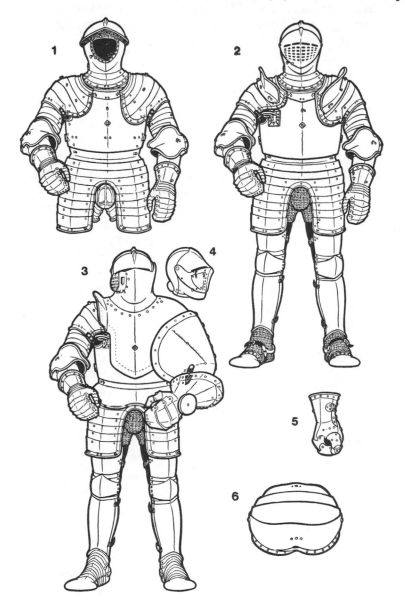

thighs and stomach. Parts of this armour are still in existence and contemporary alterations, such as additions for growth, suggest that this is the very armour made ready for the King to take with him to France in 1544.

Particularly in the tilt-armour one can see the final outcome of the 'glancing surface' principle. The cuff of the tilt gauntlet overlaps the edge of the left elbow reinforce which overlaps the lower edge of the grandguard which in turn overlaps the helmet. There are no exposed edges for an opposing lance point to catch in.

The basic field-armour of this type weighs some fifty pounds but a man in good training could still leap into the saddle without the help of the stirrups, and the idea that knights had to be hoisted on to their horses by cranes is quite untrue. For the tilt, when heavier armour was used, the combatants mounted their horses from a platform or mounting-block at the end of the lists. To a man accustomed to wear it from an early age a well-fitted armour seems to have caused little inconvenience. If he fell down in battle, unless he was actually injured or trampled on, he would be able to get up without difficulty.

The fully armoured horse had the front and sides of its head and the top of the neck covered in plates and had skirt-like plates all the way round its body. Sometimes these were decorated to match a particularly rich armour; more usually they had elaborate embroidered cloth covers laced on, which could be changed for each pageant or tournament. Horse armours of stiff prepared leather were also common because they were cheaper.

Throughout this century the spurs were riveted direct to the back of the greave when a complete armour was worn.

THE ARMY OF HENRY VIII

In the 1544 campaign the army was still divided into three main divisions the vaward or vanward, main battle, and rearward, as in the preceding century, although these were now occasionally referred to as 'regiments'. These were further divided into companies or bands of about a hundred strong, each under a captain, a petty captain, and a non-commissioned officer called a 'wiffler' or sergeant, who was a drill-instructor. Each foot company would probably have its own flag or ensign and possibly a drummer or fifer and would contain archers and handgunners as well as pikemen and billmen. Continental armies already had larger and more complicated units resembling the modern Brigade Group, such as the *Légion* in France, consisting of six companies of 1,000 men each, or the *Tercio* in Spain, consisting of ten or twelve companies of 240 men each. Occasionally small groups of companies were combined temporarily in the English army, under a special commander called a 'grand captain'.

On ceremonial occasions, such as the review of the London militia in 1539 when the army marched past the King at Westminster Palace, it was in three divisions. In the first two the handgunners and artillery marched in front, preceded by their banners

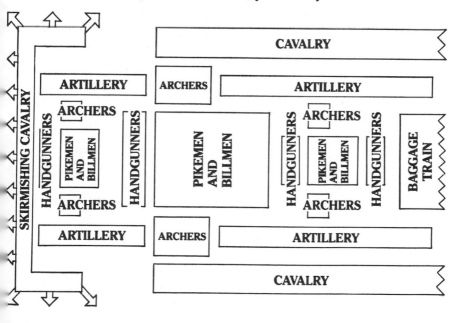

The army of Henry VIII on the march

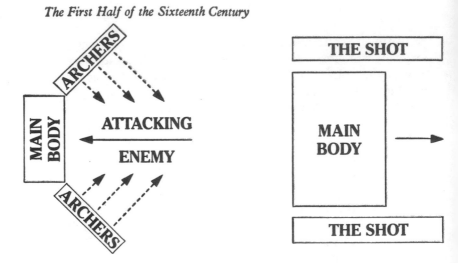

Left, formation used at Crécy. *Right,* attack formation used by
Henry VIII's army

and followed successively by the bowmen, pikemen, and billmen.
The officers were all guarded by halberdiers. In the final division
the shot came last, so as to form the rear-guard. The 16,000 men
were carefully picked so that only those owning plate armour took
part; those having only brigandines and jacks were excused duty
for the day. Every man had a sword and dagger.

The presence of a considerable number of pikemen and handgunners among the militia, who had to provide their own arms and
drill in their spare time, shows that the King's efforts to modernise
his forces were working.

The cavalry of the army of 1544 was also divided into bands of
a hundred men – mostly, of course, light horsemen. Their flag was
a guidon, originally apparently the flag of the mounted archers in
the old Burgundian Army. Companies of arquebusiers on horseback are mentioned, and many of the foreign mercenary cavalry
were no longer heavily armed lancers but *Reiters*. These were
armed with a brace or two of heavy pistols, a sword, and sometimes
a light spear.

T When on the march in open country the army formed up in its
three 'regiments', one behind the other, each consisting of a large

Two of Henry VIII's armoured cars

central block of pikemen and billmen preceded by a body of hand-gunners and flanked by a group of archers. A body of handgunners brought up the rear. The artillery was drawn by teams of horses on both flanks of the army. Bodies of cavalry formed a screen down each side of the army, skirmished in front of it, and surrounded the baggage-train, cattle, and camp followers who trailed behind. The flags, bearing either the cross of St. George or designs based on the Tudor livery colours, were placed in the centre of each division and were guarded by halberdiers.

In attack the shot formed up on each side of the main body, occasionally forming wings not unlike those at Crécy to enfilade an attacking foe. There are a number of references to armoured cars, and one drawing shows an English army accompanied by them. These were box-like structures on wheels with a battle-mented top like a tiny castle. They were propelled by a horse or horses placed between the wheels, and protected by the sides of the cart. The top was filled with handgunners. The immediate inspira-tion for these probably came from the Scots, who used them in the campaign of 1523, but ultimately they derive from the armoured wagons of the Hussite Wars in Bohemia (1420–1434).

UNIFORM IN THE FIRST HALF OF THE SIXTEENTH CENTURY

The wearing of uniform became much more common in this cen-tury. The 300 Yeomen of the Guard at the marriage of Arthur, Prince of Wales, to Catherine of Aragon in 1501 were dressed in

the Tudor livery colours of green and white in vertical stripes, embroidered with a red rose within a vine wreath on breast and back. All were armed with halberds on that occasion. Later illustrations, such as the painting of Henry VIII at the 'Field of Cloth of Gold', show a red uniform with black bars at the edges and on the arms; the badge on the breast is a rose and crown in gold. The modern uniform is a much-modified version of this. Only the livery coat was uniform at first, and illustrations show that hats and hose of different colours were worn. On active service and for guard duty there was a rust-coloured uniform.

The Yeomen were divided into archers and halberdiers, and both bodies occasionally served on horseback; the halberdiers then carried 'javelins' or boar-spears.

The normal identifying sign of an English soldier was the red cross of St. George on a white ground, and Henry himself landed in France in 1544 wearing over his armour a garment of white cloth of gold with a red cross. Illustrations often show the tunics entirely of white with the red cross in the centre; others show the red cross on part of the clothing. Usually the red cross, the King's badge, was worn together with the badge of the captain of the company. In 1513 the soldiers sent to serve in ships by the city of Canterbury had the Cornish choughs of the City coat-of-arms on their breasts and backs; in 1522 the men of Shrewsbury were issued with coats with leopards' heads on them; and the horsemen sent to the Scottish border in 1542 by the City of Coventry had the badge of an elephant on their jackets. In the London Muster of 1539 all the soldiers had coats of white over their armour with the arms of the City on the back and front, and all wore white hats

Javelin

Two of Henry VIII's soldiers of about 1535

with a feather and white hose. On this occasion the Mayor and aldermen wore black.

In 1543 the King demanded from the City of Norwich for the French war '40 able footmen, whereof 8 to be archers every one furnished with a good bow and a cace to cary it in, with 24 good arrows, a good sword, and a dagger, and the rest to be billmen well harnessed [i.e. armoured] every one of them with a good bill, a good sword and a dagger'. The men were chosen by the constables from those liable for service, and a description of their uniforms has survived. The coat was to be of blue, garded (i.e. edged and decorated) with red, after the fashion of infantrymen's coats made at London, and the left sleeve to be trimmed in such a way as it pleased the captain to devise, provided always that no gentleman or yeoman wore any kind of badge. Their right hose was to be all red, the left to be blue with a broad red stripe down the outside of the leg. Each man was to be provided with an arming doublet of fustian or canvas and every man was to have a hat to cover his helmet of a special kind made by William Tailours, capper of London,

165

for eightpence a piece. Not only were the colours laid down but the pattern was sometimes precisely stipulated. A letter survives giving exact details about how the coats of the Cambridge contingent were to be cut for the same expedition, and the writer says that he has caused a coat to be cut out and tacked together so that the authorities might know what the fashion was.

The first real effort to have the entire army uniformly dressed took place in 1547 when the Duke of Somerset informed those appointed to furnish soldiers for the expedition into Scotland that their coats were all to be red. On other occasions during the short reign of Edward VI companies are described as wearing uniforms of their captain's livery colours and badges.

ARMS IN THE FIRST HALF OF THE SIXTEENTH CENTURY

The handguns of the German mercenaries of Henry's early wars would have had heavy wooden stocks only sloping down very slightly behind the barrel. The firing position was much as it is today but the butt did not rest against the shoulder, and the kick

PRESSURE ON 'A' RELEASES THE SERPENTINE

German mercenary handgunner about 1505

German matchlock gun, about 1550

was taken up by the strength of the arms. By the middle of the century some German guns had rather longer butts which began to look quite like a modern gun and which could be rested against the shoulder. By this time the name 'hackbut' or 'arquebus' seems to have been used for these as well as for the shorter cavalry guns.

The loading procedure was exactly the same as for the cannon described earlier, the powder being poured in from a powder-flask or horn and rammed firmly home with a piece of paper, the wad, on top to keep it in position. The ball was then rammed home on top of this. The ramrod was carried in a series of loops under the stock. Once the barrel was loaded the pan was primed with finer powder from a second smaller flask, the pan-cover was closed, and the glowing slow-match placed in the serpentine. To avoid accidents the match was usually removed during reloading and held in the left hand, while the right hand did all the loading. Before firing it might be necessary to adjust the match again, and the pan-cover would have to be opened.

The Germans often carried a series of small leather or wooden bottles on a collar or bandolier, each containing enough powder for one charge. This was found to be quicker and prevented the gun from being overloaded. Since barrels were made in many sizes each gun was provided with its own mould with which to make the right size of bullet.

The matchlock remained the almost universal military lock for infantry but for expensive sporting guns and for cavalry weapons a newly invented lock was preferred. This was the wheel-lock, possibly invented by Leonardo da Vinci, the great Italian artist and engineer. It worked on the principle of a modern cigarette-lighter; the spark to light the powder was made by a wheel with a rough

Diagram of wheel-lock action

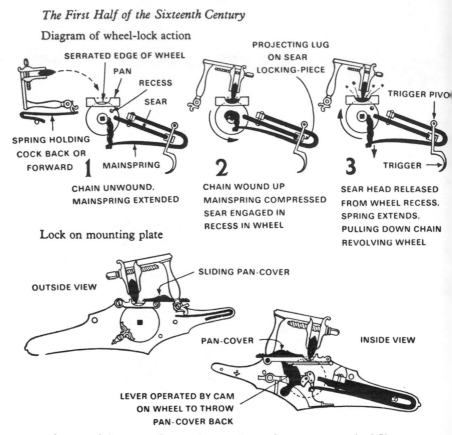

SERRATED EDGE OF WHEEL

PAN

RECESS

SEAR

PROJECTING LUG
ON SEAR

LOCKING-PIECE

TRIGGER PIVOT

SPRING HOLDING
COCK BACK OR
FORWARD **1** MAINSPRING

2

3 TRIGGER →

CHAIN UNWOUND.
MAINSPRING EXTENDED

CHAIN WOUND UP
MAINSPRING COMPRESSED
SEAR ENGAGED IN
RECESS IN WHEEL

SEAR HEAD RELEASED
FROM WHEEL RECESS.
SPRING EXTENDS.
PULLING DOWN CHAIN
REVOLVING WHEEL

Lock on mounting plate

OUTSIDE VIEW

SLIDING PAN-COVER

PAN-COVER

INSIDE VIEW

LEVER OPERATED BY CAM
ON WHEEL TO THROW
PAN-COVER BACK

edge revolving very fast against a piece of stone. Instead of flint, a softer stone, iron pyrites, was used.

To prepare the gun for action the wheel was wound up against a strong spring by means of a spanner which fitted over the axle of the wheel. Turning the axle wound round it a small length of chain which was attached to one end of a strong V-shaped spring. This compressed the spring. The wheel was then locked in the wound position. The priming powder was placed in a pan on top of the wheel and alongside the vent of the barrel. The pan-cover was closed, and the pyrites, held in a pair of plier-like jaws, was lowered on top of the pan-cover.

When the trigger was pressed the wheel was released and began to spin. A fraction of a second later the pan-cover was automatically knocked open, and the iron pyrites fell on to the spinning wheel, causing a shower of sparks which ignited the priming powder.

This system was surer than the matchlock, in which the wind could blow the powder out of the open pan and the rain could put out the match. It was easier to manage on horseback since the weapon could be carried in a holster attached to the saddle, which a lighted matchlock could not. From about 1530 onwards very short guns, later to be called 'pistols', were frequently used by the light cavalry. These and the three-foot-long weapons of the mounted arquebusiers were fired by wheel-locks. This lock was never widely adopted for infantry because it was expensive and easily broken by rough use. The average person of that period might pass his whole life without any experience of mechanics, whereas today the very youngest learn not to overwind clockwork toys.

Perhaps because of doubts about whether the wheel-lock would fire, the pistol was often combined with another weapon, and maces and warhammers sometimes had a hollow shaft acting as a pistol barrel. Swords were also fitted with a small pistol and, for hunting, crossbows were occasionally combined with a wheel-lock gun.

After 1530 the wearing of the sword with civilian dress became much more common, and instead of quarrels being settled in the lists in full armour duelling with swords came into fashion. Since the opponents were unarmoured, a lighter blade could be used than on the military weapon. In order to protect the unarmoured hand of the duellist, complicated guards were developed in front

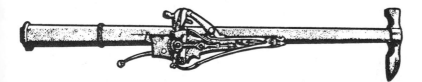

Horseman's hammer and wheel-lock pistol combined

169

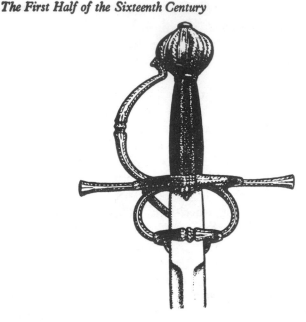

Hilt of a civilian sword (rapier) about 1550. (Wallace Collection, London)

of the cross-guards and on each side of the hand. The figure shows a fully developed sword of about 1550. There were, however, many other varieties of hilt, depending on the taste of the user or the master who taught him. Parries were usually made with the left hand or with the cloak wrapped round the arm but by the middle of the century a parrying dagger was often held, point forwards, in the left hand. The science of duelling was developed in Italy and could be learnt from Italian fencing-masters or from the books they wrote. The name 'rapier' was at first given to any civilian sword and only later came to mean a thrusting weapon when these became almost universal. Italian, and later Spanish, masters taught that the point was more deadly than the edge. The thrust became the main means of attack.

Courtiers imported expensive swords with hilts of chiselled steel, or of gold and silver decorated with jewels or coloured

Duellists, one with sword and cloak, the other with sword
and dagger

enamels. The sword and dagger began to be part of fashionable
dress, used rather to display the taste and wealth of the owner
than for offence. The King brought over foreign designers and
craftsmen to prepare rich weapons for him. Hans Holbein, whose
portraits bring Henry's court alive for us, also designed jewels,
gold state cups, and weapons for the King.

The ordinary Englishman, who always distrusted foreign novel-
ties, stuck to his broadsword and buckler.

Military sword, about 1530

171

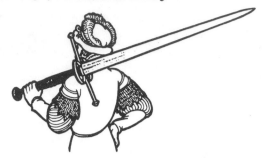

Two-handed sword, about 1530

The military sword carried by the English was usually a single-handed, two-edged, cutting or cut-and-thrust weapon with simple guards – often only the medieval cross-guard, usually with the ends curved towards the blade. However, under the influence of civilian hilts, additional guards in front of the hand became increasingly popular. Two-handed swords were used by 'wifflers' and by the guards to the flags of some companies. They were two-edged with straight blades about fifty inches long with a handle of twenty inches. The guard was usually a simple long cross flanked on each side by an open ring. For close-quarters the blade could be grasped by the right hand in front of the guards, where the blade was often covered in leather to prevent the hand from being cut. The blades of most of these military swords were imported from the

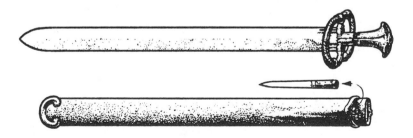

German infantry sword and sheath, about 1515

172

great manufacturing centres such as Solingen in Germany. Two-handed swords were also used for foot-combats in the tournament.

Henry's German mercenaries would have carried the single-handed swords with broad two-edged blades and with cross-guards twisted round into a figure of eight, typical of the Swiss and German *Landsknecht* regiments. An English writer noted that the Scots also preferred very broad, slashing swords.

The fashionable daggers used during Henry's reign were in the Swiss style popularised by the King himself, usually with a hilt shaped like a capital 'I' in cast metal decorated with faces and strapwork and with a heavily ornamented metal scabbard. About the middle of the century Scottish daggers were reported as being fashionable, and among the rich a dagger made to match the sword became popular. It had a plain cross-guard with a single ring-guard on the outside.

The pike or 'Morris pike' (meaning Moorish), as it was called in England, consisted of a leaf-shaped steel head fitted to a sixteen- or twenty-foot-long ash pole. So that the head could not be hacked off, it was made with two long tongues of steel, which were nailed down the sides of the shaft. The grip was bound with cloth or leather to prevent the hand from slipping, and the rear end was bound with steel to stop it splitting. The English held their pikes at waist height parallel to the ground. In action only the front three or four ranks held their pikes at the ready; the rear ranks held

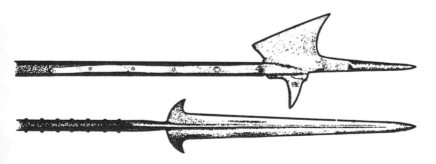

Halberd and partisan, about 1520

173

theirs upright until it was time to step forward and replace a fallen comrade.

The bill was exceptionally popular. The head was heavy, and the shaft was quite short, about six foot, because the English liked close-quarter fighting. At Flodden the English soon had the Scots at a disadvantage by chopping off their pikeheads with their stout bills. The Venetian ambassador described Henry's infantry on another occasion as carrying halberds and great clubs set with steel spikes. The halberds were cleaver-like axes on seven-foot shafts with a long stout spike on the top and a shorter one at the back of the blade. The advantage of combining halberdiers or bill-men with pikemen was that when the pikemen were halted and

Horseman's hammer, about 1560 (Victoria and Albert Museum)

could only poke at the armoured fronts of their enemies, their companions could rush out between them and hew a path through the enemy ranks.

The King's guard carried 'partisans' with gilt heads. These were spears with very broad and long blades, often with pointed lugs curving out from the base of the blade.

The crossbow continued to be used as a sporting weapon for all types of game throughout the century, and it was still used in East Anglia and the north country until well into the nineteenth century.

TACTICS IN THE FIRST HALF OF THE SIXTEENTH CENTURY

T

The only pitched battle fought with Henry's reorganised forces took place after his death. The Protector, Duke of Somerset, invaded Scotland in an attempt to force the little Queen of Scots to marry the young Edward VI – 'The War of the Rough Wooing', as the Scots called it. The English still mustered only some 600 hand-gunners and the King's Spears, and the 500 regular cavalry of the Boulogne garrison brought over for the campaign had to be reinforced by foreign mercenary cavalry and mounted arquebusiers. The light horse of the Borders were of little use in pitched battles although excellent for reconnaissance and for harrying stragglers.

The Scots were drawn up in three great blocks of pikemen on the steep bank of the River Esk at Musselburgh. Their left flank rested on an artillery earthwork near the mouth of the river. The Scottish cavalry were drawn up on the right flank but, heavily outnumbered by the enemy and demoralised by a defeat on the previous day, they took no part in the battle. This flank was, however, also protected by a marsh. Thus the only way the English could attack was from the front. This they prepared to do. Since they had an immense superiority in number and weight of guns and of cavalry, they probably intended to bombard the Scots until, their ranks broken, the latter could be overrun by the cavalry. The Scots, however, did not wait to be attacked but rushed at the English while the latter were marching along the opposite bank in order to get into position. The guns of the English fleet opened fire on the left flank of the Scots, driving off the Highland archers and forcing the nearest body of pikemen to move inland out of range. As the Scots crossed the river and began to climb the steep bank opposite, their charge began to slow down, giving Somerset time to face his army towards them. But, if the English were to gain any advantage from their artillery and missile weapons, the Scots must be stopped altogether from closing. Somerset halted them by throwing in his heavy cavalry in two desperate and costly charges. It was like Bannockburn all over again; the English horse fell in swathes without breaking the wall of pikes but the Scots charge was halted. The artillery and small shot began to smash into the ranks of the stationary and defenceless pikemen. Unable to advance, they fell slowly back and then fled, pursued by the exultant English cavalry.

Chapter Eight

The Second Half of the Sixteenth Century

ORGANISATION AND THE ARMY IN THE SECOND HALF OF THE SIXTEENTH CENTURY

Queen Mary may have lost Calais but she did a great deal to improve the defences of England. In 1558 the ancient Statute of Winchester was abolished, and a new standard of arms and arming was laid down for all classes. All those who had land worth £1,000 a year or more were to keep six horse for demilances, three of which were to have suitable harness and armour for the riders; ten horses suitable for light horsemen, with the necessary harness and the armour for the men; forty corslets – that is, infantry cuirasses with full arms, tassets, and open helmets; forty lighter armours for footmen, called 'almain rivets' or, instead, forty coats of plates or brigandines; forty pikes; thirty longbows, each with twenty-four arrows; thirty light steel caps; twenty bills and halberds; twenty arquebuses; and, finally, twenty morions. Each class below this rank had to produce horses and equipment in proportion to their income, down to those with between £5 and £10 a year who had to provide only one coat of plates; one bill or halberd; one bow with its arrows; and one light helmet. Those who had no land were assessed according to the value of their goods or cattle. The inhabitants of all towns, parishes, and hamlets had to provide such arms and armour as their Majesties' Commissioners appointed. Inventories were to be drawn up of all this armour, and it was to be inspected at intervals to make sure that it was not being sold or allowed to rot. The sale of any of this armour was absolutely forbidden.

The Lieutenant of Henry VIII's reign became the Lord Lieutenant, usually appointed for a single shire. He took over the leadership of the militia from the sheriff. It was now his duty to muster and organise the shire, appointing its officers, and reviewing and listing the armour with the help of the local Commissioners. Since Lord Lieutenants were usually members of the Queen's Council they could be more closely supervised than the sheriff.

Soldiers who failed to turn up at the muster or came without their armour were to be fined. Officers appointed to hold musters were absolutely forbidden to take money for releasing men whose names were on the muster roll, under the pain of a fine of ten times what they received. Officers were not allowed to release men once they were levied, and they were ordered to pay them within ten days.

Unfortunately, no attempt was made to reorganise the call-up of troops for overseas service. The semi-feudal forces raised by landowners were no longer used, and no further effort was made to raise a regular army like Edward VI's short-lived bands of 'gendarmery'. The only forces to survive were the two Royal Guards and the reorganised militia. Strictly speaking, the militia could not legally be forced to serve overseas, but when the need was great, men were conscripted and only a few lawyers complained.

When forces were required for expeditions to Ireland or the Continent the Lord Lieutenant was commissioned to choose sufficient suitable men from the militia of the whole shire. Volunteers came forward from the more adventurous, from those who hoped to make money by plunder, and from those whose criminal activities had made life in their home county rather too warm. The remainder of the force was made up of conscripted men chosen by the local Commissioners assisting the Lord Lieutenant. The fear of leaving the country defenceless meant that the trained men of the militia, who were the most suitable for the army, were exempted from conscription. Efforts were made to solve the chronic unemployment by rounding up all the able-bodied unemployed and enlisting them.

In spite of the new law, this system was used to feather the nests of the recruiting officers, sheriffs, and justices of the peace, who would enlist yeomen and well-to-do householders with no desire to serve at all. These would then pay richly for their release, and, for a small sum, a substitute would be bought from among the great body of unemployed and unemployable who roamed Tudor England. Falstaff's recruiting party in Shakespeare's *Henry IV*, *Part I* is an example of this sort of corruption at work. Latterly, the names and descriptions of the men, their arms and armour, and their horses, if it was a cavalry troop, were written down to prevent this sort of substitution.

The commander of the force was appointed by the Queen but the junior officers, appointed by the Lord Lieutenant, tended to be either old professionals, well-schooled in fleecing their men, or young gentlemen of the county, totally untrained in war.

Naturally, under such conditions, discipline was non-existent and desertion very common; the men, unaccustomed to campaign life, died like flies, and the companies, or such of them as were still alive, had to be trained on arrival in the field. Companies on campaign which should have had about 150 men were always under-strength because it was very difficult for captains to get new recruits from home, and because dishonest captains failed to report men lost by death or desertion so that they could pocket their pay and clothing allowances. Sickness was rife since, although each company had a surgeon, the pay of twenty pence a day was not enough to attract skilled men. Captains often provided much cheaper uniforms than they should have done, and poor quality food. In winter the men froze in their ragged uniforms and starved on rotten food.

Military writers of the time complained about all these faults of the system, and by the end of the reign a good many improvements had been introduced into the organisation of armies raised for overseas service.

A better recruiting system was often used, in which individual captains of tried ability were commissioned to raise companies of volunteers. In this case, since they were actually going to have to lead them into action, they chose the best available men and armed and equipped them as well as possible.

The shortage of men in individual companies on service was tackled in two ways. Firstly, by very strict inspections of the muster rolls and the men at irregular intervals by an officer called the muster-master, to see that the number of men present corresponded with the number the Queen was paying for. Secondly, officers were made responsible for keeping up their numbers and were allowed an extra man's wages for a month to pay for recruiting, transporting, and equipping each new recruit. The organisation of the companies into regiments of ten companies, under the command of an officer called a 'colonel', helped to keep dishonest captains at bay. Latterly, a second-in-command, called a 'lieutenant colonel', was appointed to assist the commander.

The replacement of the company surgeons by two qualified regimental surgeons, each paid five shillings a day, lessened the losses due to illness, since it attracted more skilful men, and they could afford to pay one or two trainees whose work they would supervise.

The organisation of ranks was complex but moving towards modern methods. During the first Netherlands expedition, the commander, the Earl of Leicester, was called 'Lieutenant and Captain-general', while his successor was called 'Sergeant-major General and Colonel-general'. The second-in-command of the army, the 'High-marshal', was assisted by the 'Provost-marshal' who looked after discipline, the lay-out of the camp, and the order of march. The horse and foot were each commanded by a general, the artillery by the Master of the Ordnance, and there was a Sergeant-Major whose task was to draw up the army in line of battle; this was a much higher rank than the present-day sergeant-major.

At company level, the Captain was assisted by two other officers, a lieutenant, and an ensign who carried the company flag. There were two sergeants, two drummers who acted as messengers and signallers, and six corporals each responsible for the drill of a part of the company. Attached to each company there were usually about four gentleman-volunteers who served unpaid, or for whatever the Captain allowed them, in the hope of gaining a commission in the field for gallantry. About the time of the Armada rather more than half the infantry company consisted of pikemen but, by the end of the century, the handgunners formed over half the numbers. The trained bands of London, Cambridge, Huntingdon, and Wiltshire, when mustered for the Armada, did not include a single bowman; but those of more distant counties consisted of up to a third of archers.

Pay was the responsibility of the Treasurer at War, each of whom seems to have made a huge, and partly illegal, profit. Although the money was usually late, the men received it personally from the assistants of the Treasurer at War, thus preventing captains from withholding pay illegally or drawing it for corpses or deserters. Officially, captains were allowed pay for five to ten non-existent men in order to increase their own pay and to reward deserving soldiers; this was supposed to be strictly accounted for. The pay of a captain was eight shillings a day; of a lieutenant, four shillings; of an ensign, two shillings; of a drummer or trumpeter, twenty pence; of a cavalryman, eighteen pence a day; and of an infantryman, eightpence.

Better quality uniforms were provided by government, though officers and clothiers alike conspired to cheat the men of their due.

In order to cut down desertion, all soldiers going on leave were issued with passes to show the constables if they were challenged as deserters. Six weeks' annual leave was allowed but no more than six men might be absent from a company at one time.

One of the major difficulties of calling up a better class of man, the yeoman and craftsman, was the additional unemployment caused at the disbandment of an army after a campaign. By law their previous employers were supposed to take the men back; in fact this was rarely possible and they joined the army of sturdy beggars and vagrants. In 1590 the authorities at seaports where soldiers were disembarking were ordered to list all returning men and give them sufficient money to return to their place of muster, and passes which allowed them time to get home but without which they might be arrested as vagrants. Thereafter it was the responsibility of his parish to look after the man until he found a job. If he was permanently disabled he was paid a pension from the parish poor rate. In fact, sixteenth-century organisation was not capable of dealing with a problem so vast, and the system was never fully workable.

In 1572 an act was passed for the improvement of the militia, which was really the reintroduction of selective service as in Saxon times. A convenient number of able-bodied men were to be chosen and sorted into companies to be trained and drilled at the expense of the county. This is the origin of the 'trained bands'. They were not fully trained men but men to be trained, and this was their failing. When Sir John Norris saw the raw troops gathered to repel the Spanish veterans of the Armada in 1588, 'he wondered that he could see no man in the kingdom afeared but himself'. Since the men of the trained bands were immune from conscription they became a refuge for shirkers.

The type of troops forming Elizabeth's army remained much the same as in her father's day. It was becoming more and more difficult to find men properly trained as archers. On strenuous campaigns sickness and poor food made even these too weak to use their bows, but as long as a man could drag himself to his feet he could still fire a gun. In 1595, after a fierce battle of pamphlets between those who believed in the handgun and the supporters of the longbow, the bow was finally abolished as a weapon in the trained bands and the regular army.

Illustrations of the English army in Ireland in 1581 show that the cavalry were of two kinds. The heavy horseman wore cuirass with tassets to mid-thigh; full arms; and comb-morion, which had a ridge running fore and aft over the skull and steel-covered ear-flaps tied under the chin. They were armed with swords and with heavy lances without hand-guards. The light horse had comb-morion and mail shirt; they carried a sword and a light lance. The legs of all the cavalry were protected only by high leather boots. In 1584 the light cavalry of the City of Norwich were to have a pair of pistols in cases on their saddles, and jacks of plate, or brigandines. Many out-of-date armours were cut up to make jacks for the

SHOT   HALBERDIER   PIKEMAN   LIGHT HORSE   HEAVY HORSE

The English Army in Ireland, 1581

Navy.

The pikemen in Ireland wore cuirasses, full arms, and comb-morions and carried pike, sword, and dagger. The halberdiers who guarded the company flags were similarly armoured but some-times did without the arms; they carried halberd, sword, and dagger. The shot were all arquebusiers and wore no armour except the comb-morion. As well as their firearm they had a sword and dagger; they carried a flask of powder on a shoulder-belt, together with a smaller flask for the priming powder.

The trumpeters of the cavalry, and the drummers and fifers of the infantry, wore no armour but carried swords and daggers. In other illustrations officers are distinguished by the richness of their dress and armour, and by carrying a boat-spear or short pike as a sign of their rank. They are often shown accompanied by a page carrying their round shield. This was a fashion introduced from Spain where 'targets', as these shields were called, were used, partly in imitation of the Roman shield-carrying legionaries and

Elizabethan captain of infantry. His page carries his shield

partly in order to break into the ranks of pikemen by using the shield to push aside the points. Prince Maurice of Orange, the Protestant leader, armed some of his men with bullet-proof targets as protection against musket fire when they were advancing to the attack.

0 UNIFORM IN THE SECOND HALF OF THE SIXTEENTH CENTURY

The soldier going overseas was issued with his first uniform at the muster where he was levied. It was paid for out of county funds with a small government subsidy. At first it consisted only of a coat, usually of a uniform colour; like the forty billmen of Reading, in 1556, who had blue coats with red crosses, each coat costing six shillings and fourpence. The men of different counties continued to be dressed differently, and the uniforms issued by a county in different years were not necessarily the same. Latterly, some counties provided their levies with a full suit of clothes. Twice a year government issued uniforms consisting of a 'cassock' (a sort of overcoat), a doublet, a pair of peg-topped knee-breeches called 'venetians', a hat, two shirts, and three pairs each of shoes and stockings. Officers were also issued with their uniforms, which were of rather better quality than the men's. Later government bought in bulk from large-scale contractors who, with an assured outlet, could undercut their competitors. The army should have gained by getting its clothing cheaper and, no doubt, bulk-buying did lead to uniformity of dress. Complaints of shoddy uniforms not as good as those patterns kept in the Wardrobe Office were constant, and no doubt, like everyone else at the time, the clothing inspectors could be bribed to pass bad workmanship and cheap cloth. Red and blue were the most popular colours for army coats, usually edged with strips of some other colour. A red cap was very often worn, sometimes over the steel skull-cap.

TOURNAMENTS IN THE SECOND HALF OF THE SIXTEENTH CENTURY

The most famous tournaments of Elizabeth's reign were the annual celebrations of the Queen's Accession on 17 November. The Queen's Champion and other members of her court enacted an elaborate charade in which Elizabeth herself was the heroine. As we might expect in the age of Sir Philip Sidney and Edmund Spenser, the ceremony was exceptionally elaborate and was closely interwoven with a pastoral allegory glorifying England's Queen and the Protestant faith. It was part of a cult which helped to bind Catholic and Protestant together and give them a common loyalty in their devotion to the Virgin Queen. The speeches, of which there were many, were filled with literary allusions. The knights wore disguises over their armour; on one occasion Sir Philip Sidney was a shepherd, another knight was a savage dressed in leaves,

185

a third was a 'Frozen Knight' in armour made to look like ice. They carried cardboard shields painted with symbolic devices, which they gave up before the tilt. Their armour and horse coverings were decorated with the initials and badges of their ladies. For instance, Sidney had stars on his armour in honour of Stella Rich. For the country people it was a holiday, taking the place of the older church holidays, now abolished. They paid an entry fee of twelve pence to watch.

The combats usually consisted of a tilt with blunt lances, a course at random with blunt swords, and finally a foot-combat with blunt pike and sword over a barrier. The heralds kept the score on specially prepared score-sheets. At first, blows on the head counted more than blows on the body, while a glancing blow counted least. If the lance was broken it counted extra. If the rider struck his opponent's saddle or the tilt he lost marks. Late in Elizabeth's reign a less complicated system was introduced in which all blows counted equally. The score for the course at random was kept in the same way, and extra marks were given for striking off a gauntlet. At the barriers it was the breaking of weapons that counted. For this last combat only the cuirass, arms, shoulders, gauntlets, gorget, and close-helmet were worn.

ARMOUR IN THE SECOND HALF OF THE SIXTEENTH CENTURY

The armour of the second half of the sixteenth century differed from the earlier type principally in the shape, which followed that of fashionable costume. The breastplate was first made longer, and the waist dipped at the front to below the natural waistline. The skirt and tassets began to swell out to leave room for the fashionable puffed short trousers. By 1580 the 'peascod' breastplate had come in from Italy. The waistline became sharply pointed downwards at the centre and was overhung by a hump-like projection of the breastplate. As the short pants became fuller, so the skirt and tassets had to bulge out further. The ridge running fore and aft over the top of the helmet tended to get higher and

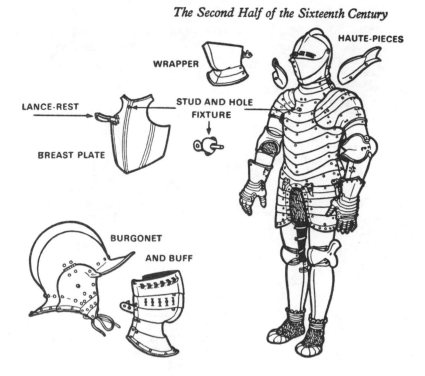

A small Greenwich garniture of Mary's reign

higher as time went on. The feet were made more or less in the natural shape of the foot but without distinction of left or right.

Many English portraits show that the nobility were importing expensive and highly decorated armours from Italy, Germany, and France. Many gentlemen of the court were allowed to have armours made for them by the royal armourers at Greenwich.

The normal Greenwich field-armour of Mary's reign had a close-helmet rotating on the gorget; full arms; breast and back, some-times made of many horizontal plates riveted together loosely to allow the wearer to move more freely; short tassets; cuisses (thigh defences), also made of many overlapping lames; poleyns and greaves. The feet were usually protected by mail shoes with steel toe-caps. The gauntlets had separate fingers, each covered by a

187

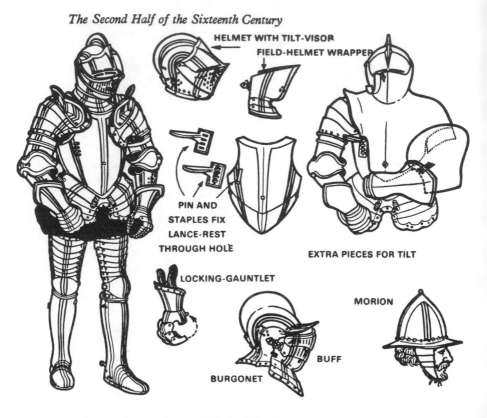

HELMET WITH TILT-VISOR

FIELD-HELMET WRAPPER

PIN AND
STAPLES FIX
LANCE-REST
THROUGH HOLE

EXTRA PIECES FOR TILT

LOCKING-GAUNTLET

MORION

BUFF

BURGONET

A Greenwich garniture of Elizabeth's reign

series of steel scales. There would be a number of additional pieces; a heavy breastplate with a lance-rest attached to wear over the first one; a wrapper with gorget plates to wear as additional protection for the lower part of the helmet and the gorget; and, finally, often a second helmet, open-faced but with a face-guard which could be put on if required.

Armours intended for use in the tilt-yard, as well as for battle, had solid breasts and backs and even more additional pieces. These are a second, heavier visor for the close-helmet; a grand-guard to cover the left shoulder and the lower part of the front of the helmet; a large reinforce for the left elbow; and a very heavy

188

An armour of the Emperor Charles V made in imitation of a Roman armour. Dated 1546 (Royal Armoury, Madrid)

gauntlet for the left hand. All these were used in the tilt with blunt lances. For the mounted combat with blunt swords and the dismounted combat over a barrier a right locking-gauntlet was provided. There were removable haute-pieces for the foot-combat or for the field, if the owner wished. Usually a saddle and a small chanfron were also provided, all decorated to match.

Later in the century more complicated sets were made, but the most important new pieces were the morion and round shield used by infantry officers in the fashionable Spanish style. Some armours were made with lighter arms, consisting only of shoulder defences extending a little further than before down the upper arm. These would be worn over mail sleeves and with gauntlets with long cuffs reaching almost to the elbows. Haute-pieces had now disappeared

189

and plate shoes were once more fashionable. The person ordering one of these Greenwich armours could presumably choose what pieces he required. Some had only light-horse armours, others had one of the very complicated sets. In 1614 a complete Greenwich armour for the field and tilt for Henry, Prince of Wales, cost £340.

For pageants, armours were made like those worn by Roman statues of generals, with the cuirass embossed to look like the muscles of the body and with the skirts of leather straps copied in steel. A contemporary drawing of a scene in one of Shakespeare's plays, *Titus Andronicus*, shows armours of this type in wear.

ARMS IN THE SECOND HALF OF THE SIXTEENTH CENTURY

The illustrations of the English army in Ireland show the shot all armed with the fairly light handguns with downward curved stock. These may have been arquebuses or a new weapon, the 'caliver' (so called because it was of uniform *calibre* throughout the army), which was just replacing the older weapon. On the Continent, a larger gun called a 'musket' had been developed. This had a longer barrel and fired a heavier ball over a greater distance. It could pierce all but the very heaviest armour and could be used at longer ranges than earlier handguns. The increase of weight meant that the barrel had to be supported on a forked rest while the gun was being fired. On the march this rest was used as a walking stick. The musket was apparently introduced into England by the 1560's,

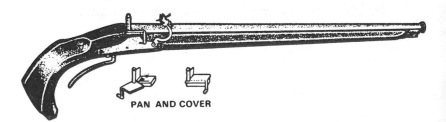

PAN AND COVER

Matchlock arquebus or caliver, about 1580

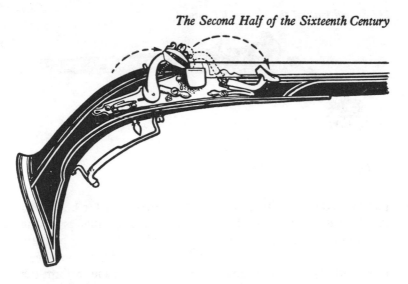

Snaphaunce sporting gun, English, about 1580

and an illustration of the funeral of Sir Philip Sidney (1587) shows musketeers; they are wearing bandoliers with charges of powder in little wooden, or leather, bottles.

The handguns used by the infantry all appear to have been simple matchlocks with the long sear-lever rather than a trigger. Although the musket usually fired a ball of lead, small steel arrows with a wad at the back were occasionally used.

The sporting guns of the well-to-do were usually wheel-locks but by the middle of the century a new system, the snaphaunce, was coming into use. This used the contemporary method of striking a light by knocking a piece of flint against a piece of steel. On the gunlock the flint was placed in a pair of jaws, called the 'cock', pivoted on the side of the lock plate. The steel was fixed on the end of a pivoted arm, and could be swung over the top of the pan where it formed a vertical wall immediately over the powder. The cock was pulled back against the force of a strong spring and locked into position automatically. Pressing the trigger released the cock which swung forward, knocking the flint sharply against the face of the steel and causing a shower of sparks to fall in the

191

Snaphaunce pistol, English, dated 1593

powder in the pan. On some guns the pan-cover had to be opened first by hand; on others it was opened automatically, as on the wheel-lock. By the end of the century this lock was apparently becoming popular for pistols, since it was cheaper than the wheel-lock. Latterly, the lower edge of the steel was made to form the pan-cover, and as the steel flew up with the force of the blow the pan was opened. This system was improved considerably and, as the 'flintlock', remained the normal type of lock for military guns until nearly the middle of the nineteenth century.

Continental cavalry were beginning to use cartridges to load their pistols. These were cylinders of stiff paper containing the exact charge of powder. The ends were tied off with thread like a sausage, and at one end the bullet was also tied in. To load, the cartridge was torn open at the end away from the bullet and a little of the powder poured into the pan. The remainder was poured into the barrel, and the paper and ball rammed down on top of it. The paper then acted as a wad. These cartridges were carried in a small box fixed to the waist-belt.

The sword used by the average Englishman continued to be designed principally for cutting. The military sword had usually a long cross-guard, finger-rings, and side rings, but often no knuckle-guard and none of the diagonal guards found on continental weapons. The more fashionable swordsman, however, had a hilt similar to those used at other European courts and a long, rather

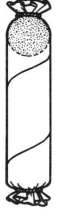

Sixteenth-century cartridge

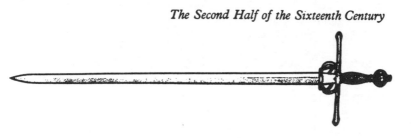

Military sword, about 1580

narrow blade, mainly for thrusting but capable of slashing an opponent's hand or face in a duel. The blade was usually imported from north Italy, from Toledo in Spain, or from Passau or Solingen in Germany and would be signed by the bladesmith, either with his full name or his trademark. Some bladesmiths signed with their own mark and the name of some more famous smith or town of manufacture, in order to take in a gullible customer. When Shakespeare made Othello say: 'It is a sword of Spain, the icebrook's temper', this is a muddled reference to such a blade, since

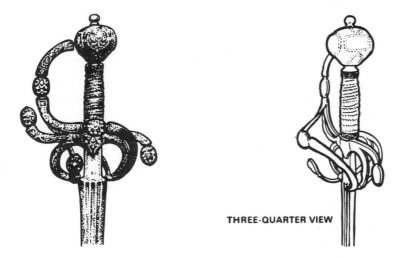

THREE-QUARTER VIEW

Sword hilt for an English courtier, about 1600. It is decorated with silver and gold (Wallace Collection, London)

193

Left-hand dagger, late sixteenth century

'ice-brook' is really Innsbruck in Austria. The blades would arrive in bundles at the swordsmith's and he would then put on them the type of hilt that his customer wanted.

These swords were used with left-hand daggers with simple cross-guards, with a ring-guard or shell on the front of the guard.

Left-hand dagger, probably English, about 1600

The sword was carried in a broad triangular sling on the waist-belt, and was kept from swinging by a diagonal strap across the stomach. The scabbard was worn almost parallel with the ground and it stuck out under the cloak behind. The ordinary person's sword still sometimes had a small knife in the scabbard, which was not usually found on the fashionable weapon.

The halberd and the bill were the only staff weapons to survive for real war but ceremonial spears, like the partisans of the Yeomen of the Guard and the polaxes of the Gentlemen-at-Arms – the two Royal bodyguards – were still used on State occasions. The 'partisan' is a broad-bladed spear with small blades curving up on each side of the main one. Usually, there were heavy tassel-like

Sword-hanger, about 1600

194

fringes just below the heads of these weapons for display, although originally they had been designed to keep rain from running down the shafts. The bill was abolished as a military weapon in 1596.

ARTILLERY AND FORTIFICATIONS IN THE SECOND HALF OF THE SIXTEENTH CENTURY

Elizabethan writers disagree about the names and sizes of big guns a little less than earlier authors, and now we can begin to divide guns into different types.

The cannon was normally the largest gun used and was intended for siege work – for smashing stone walls by the sheer weight of shot. The whole-cannon was usually a little over 7 inches in diameter inside and fired a 50-pound iron shot over a maximum range of 2,000 paces. The demi-cannon, with an internal diameter of a little over 6 inches, fired a 32-pound iron ball some 1,700 paces.

The culverin was the normal field-gun and the gun preferred by the Royal Navy by the end of the century. Guns of this type had rather lighter shot than cannons but had longer range. The whole-culverin of 5¼ inches inside diameter fired a 17-pound iron ball 2,500 paces, while the demi-culverin of 4¼ inches fired a 9-pound ball over a similar range.

Stone shot were still fired from large guns called 'Periers' which,

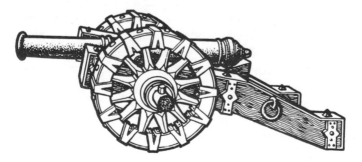

Elizabethan field-gun

because of the lighter shot requiring a smaller charge, could be made thinner in the walls. They were 8-inch guns firing a 24-pound ball but over a range of only 1,600 paces. Since they were outranged by even 5-pounder field guns, such as the saker, they were abandoned by the end of the century.

Many smaller guns were used aboard ship and on castle walls, often loaded with bags of bullets for use against attackers at short range. Sometimes the bullets were fired in a cylindrical basket instead of a bag.

One of the main reasons for the success of the Navy against the Armada was apparently that the English were armed with long-range culverins and fought out of range of the Spaniards' cannons and perriers. If the two fleets had closed in the normal fashion of that day, the English ships would have been pounded to pieces. The Spaniards also had many smaller guns to sweep the decks of any ship that came close enough to try to board.

Most, but not all, sixteenth-century guns were cast with two loops on top of the barrel at the point of balance. These were used for lifting the guns off and on to their carriages, the ropes of a crane passing through the loops.

The larger field-guns could be fired about sixty or seventy times in one day with a crew of two gunners and ten assistants; smaller guns such as falconets could be fired 140 times a day and required a much smaller crew.

Mary was aware of the danger of invasion, particularly from the north, and new defences were built at Berwick. These were of the very latest type developed in Italy. Two new principles were used. In Henry's type of fort the guns were placed along the walls of semicircular bastions so that only one or two guns could fire at the same target at one time. Now, the guns were placed so that their fire crossed the fire of other guns at the point where the enemy was expected. Although the latest type of heavy cannon could shatter a stone fort quite quickly, it was discovered that a really thick earth bank could absorb even the heaviest shot without breaking. The new walls of Berwick consisted of a very thick earth bank faced with a wall of stone, sloping back slightly. At each

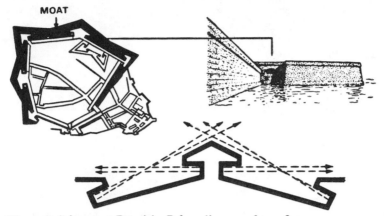

MOAT

The new defences at Berwick. *Below*, diagram of gun-fire
sweeping the front of the bastions

corner of the wall was a bastion, similarly constructed and shaped
in plan like a very broad arrow-head. From the flank of these
bastions guns placed in two tiers could sweep the length of the
walls and the ditch. The remainder of the guns were placed on the
broad platform formed by the top of the walls, and on the top of
the bastions where they were set for crossfire, covering the area in
front of the walls between bastions.

This type of bastion was still in fashion when the Spanish
Armada was threatening the shores of England: great arrowhead-
shaped bastions were built in front of the old town walls of Yar-
mouth while, a little later, a complete outer wall of this type was
built around Carisbrooke Castle in the Isle of Wight.

Chapter Nine

The Seventeenth Century up to 1660

THE ARMY, 1600 to 1660

This century saw the final triumph of firearms over armour. The commonest form of infantry firearm, the musket, fired a ball of $\frac{1}{12}$ of a pound of lead. This could pierce all but the heaviest plate, and an armour made to withstand musket shot all over would have been too heavy to wear. Armours were made with breastplates proof against muskets and with other parts proof against carbines or pistols or pikes. The soldiers complained about the weight of their armour and refused to wear it. Occasionally, the authorities were forced to provide carts or pack animals to carry the armour of their infantry on the march; at other times they had to pay the men extra to wear it; Sir Richard Hawkins describes how, on his South Sea voyage, his men 'esteemed a pott of wine a better defence than an armour of proofe . . .' Manœuvrability was thought to be a better defence against musket balls than the heaviest armour.

Great interest was taken in the Art of War and many books were written on the subject. Some of these are very interesting because they tell us about the tactics to be used in battle and siege, the forming of an encampment, the use of artillery and the types of guns, the duties of the various ranks, and the types of soldiers commonly found in the army of that day. Others are drill books giving the very numerous words of command for arms drill and, in some cases, illustrating each movement with beautiful engravings.

The heavy cavalry usually wore full armour, but with thick boots

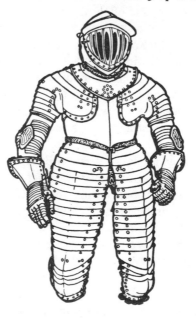

Field-armour, about 1620

in place of the greaves and plate shoes. The headpiece was usually a close-helmet, sometimes with the visor replaced by a grille of vertical bars or with a mask-like plate pierced over the eyes and mouth, both attached to a movable peak. The horse sometimes wore a chanfron, but the remainder of the horse armour and the steel plates of the saddle were abandoned in order to achieve manœuvrability. In most cases the lance was now given up, except in Spain and Scotland; some of the Scottish horse at Marston Moor (1644) were lancers. The arms of the heavy cavalry were a long sword and a pair of pistols carried in holsters on the saddle-bow. Although these heavily armed cavalry were quite common in the Thirty Years War in Germany, in the Civil War here they were most uncommon. The Earl of Essex, the Parliamentarian General, had a fully armoured troop of Life Guards, and a regiment raised for Parliament by Sir Arthur Hazelrigg was called by the Cavaliers 'the regiment of lobsters, because of their bright iron shells with which they were covered'. Cavalry armoured with a

199

breastplate, and often with an open-faced helmet, continued to be used in continental armies down to the First World War. [It was the freedom from head wounds among French cavalrymen wearing their helmets in the trenches which caused the Allied Armies to adopt a steel helmet. Body-armour for special troops was later adopted and it was worn by airmen in the Second World War, thus forging a link with the knight of the Middle Ages.]

Medium cavalry were armed similarly to the heavy cavalry but with an open-faced helmet. Light cavalry, at least in the well-organised armies of Western Europe, consisted principally of men armed with short firearms, either arquebuses or carbines (which had a smaller bore) which they fired from horseback. Although at the beginning of the century they wore a half-armour with an open-faced helmet, by the time of the Civil War only the helmet, back, breast, and a long steel gauntlet on the bridle hand survived. These were worn over a buff leather coat, thick enough to turn a sword cut, which had long skirts to protect the thighs. The cavalry of the New Model Army were all armoured in this way but at first, since they were used in the role of heavy cavalry, they carried no carbine. By the 'fifties the campaigns in Ireland and Scotland required carbiniers, so the cavalry of the New Model were issued with carbines.

The lobster-tailed helmet, with its three face-bars, which artists always show as the characteristic headpiece of the Roundheads, was worn by both sides. It is, in fact, a homely copy of a Turkish helmet first introduced into Europe some hundred years before.

At the beginning of the century a regiment of infantry consisted half of pikemen and half of musketeers or caliver men. By the time of the Civil War the caliver man had disappeared and the proportion of shot had risen to two-thirds. The pikemen remained necessary to keep the cavalry at a respectful distance from the musketeers and could not be dispensed with until the 1670's, when the introduction of the bayonet made the musketeer his own pikeman.

The illustrations of the soldiers of Prince Maurice of Orange made in 1607 for de Gheyn's drill book show the musketeers completely without armour. They wore ordinary civilian dress with

The usual armour of the
cavalryman of the Civil War;
the buff leather coat, breast
and back plates, the
bridle gauntlet and the helmet

wide-brimmed hat bedecked with ostrich feathers; over the left
shoulder was a broad belt from which hung a dozen or so wooden
bottles, each containing a single charge of powder for the musket.
Attached to the lower end of the belt were a bag of bullets, a
priming flask, and a coil of slow-match. In the left hand the musketeer held his rest, a four-foot-long pole with a steel fork at the
top to take the weight of the barrel, and spike at the bottom so
that it could be stuck in the ground for steadiness. He also carried
a long sword. The Prince's caliver men were similarly dressed but
had open-faced helmets with a high comb. They had no need of a
rest for their lighter guns which fired a bullet of seventeen or
twenty to the pound of lead. They loaded from a powder flask
hung on the right hip, and had a sword and a dagger. By the time

Musketeer of Prince Maurice of Orange's Regiments, 1607

that the New Model Army was raised (1645) the musket had been shortened in the barrel and was light enough to be used without a rest. The shoulder-belt with its small bottles of powder was very dangerous: John Gwynn, in his *Military Memoires of the Great Civil War*, writes: 'A soldier's bandolier who guarded the Colours, took fire and went off in a heat, which made an incredible confusion among us'. The bottles also rattled in the wind, which prevented

Pikeman and caliver man of Prince Maurice of Orange's
Regiments, 1607

the men from hearing the words of command or gave away surprise attacks at night. Many officers wanted them to be replaced by
cartridges carried in boxes on a waist-belt but the changeover was
not completed until after the formation of the present regular
army in 1660.

The pikemen of the Guard of the Prince of Orange – always

chosen for their height, as any little man could fire a gun but it took a well-set-up fellow to handle a pike with grace – wore a cuirass with short tassets and a helmet like that of the caliver men. When on the march the helmet was hitched to the back of the cuirass by a small hook. The pikemen wore strong leather gauntlets to protect their hands from splinters from the eighteen-foot ash staff. They too carried a sword. By the middle of the century the pikeman had largely disappeared from continental armies but he lingered on in the British Army until the beginning of the eighteenth century. Pike armour does not seem to have been much worn after 1688.

Mounted infantry were particularly useful for skirmishing and outpost duty, and for small expeditions when they could act either as light cavalry or as infantry, whichever was required. They were now called 'dragoons' after the type of light firearm they had originally carried, called a 'dragon'. Before the Civil War the dragoon regiment included musketeers and pikemen in the same proportion as in the infantry regiment, but the New Model dragoons were all musketeers. Their musket was carried hanging at their side from a shoulder-belt, and was usually fitted with a flintlock since on horseback this was easier to manage than a matchlock. Swords were issued but not pistols until later, when the dragoon had become more of a cavalryman and less of an infantryman. When they fought on foot, every eleventh man held the horses of the other ten.

The chain of command in a mid-seventeenth-century army was exceptionally complicated. At the head of the army was the General; his administrative work was done by his civilian secretary. Beneath the General was the Lieutenant General, who was second-in-command of the army and commanded the cavalry; under him were several staff officers, including his second-in-command, the Commissary-General of Horse.

Similarly, the infantry was commanded by the Sergeant Major General or Major General of Foot who, since he was in charge of drawing up the army for battle, was usually a veteran of long standing. He, too, had a staff. The Artillery and Engineers were commanded by a Lieutenant General of the Ordnance and his staff. Numerous other staff officers commanded the various administrative branches of the army, the most important of whom was the Scout Master General who was responsible for intelligence and reconnaissance.

The regiment of horse was commanded by a colonel assisted by a major. Each troop had a captain, a lieutenant, a cornet, a quartermaster, and three corporals. The cornets carried the troop flags known as 'cornets'.

The regimental flags used by the infantry on both sides in the Civil War were often more like political cartoons than proper flags; for instance, one parliamentarian regiment's flag showed a soldier threatening to kill a bishop.

However, a list of the flags of the trained bands of London, made in 1643, shows that a logical system was already in use. Each regiment had a distinctive colour for its flags. Each company had a large square flag carried by the Ensign: that of the Colonel's company was all of the regimental colour; that of the Lieutenant-Colonel was the same, but with a small St George's cross on a white square in the top corner near the pole; the Major's flag had a single distinctive mark; that of the First Captain two marks, and so on, down to the Fourth Captain who had five marks. The distinctive marks used by the White Regiment, for instance, were red diamonds.

Dragoon flags, called 'guidons', had slit ends with rounded points; the London Dragoons' five troops all had yellow flags, the different troops being distinguished by different numbers of large black dots.

The drill-books of the time describe the thirty or so separate movements, each with its own command, required to load and fire the infantryman's gun on ceremonial parades. In action these were reduced to three: 'Make ready – Present – Give fire'.

The pike drill included two different positions for receiving cavalry. For heavy cavalry, the butt of the pike was stuck in the ground and the pikeman drew his sword to defend himself if the pike shaft broke. For light cavalry, the pikeman held his pike at

Left, First Captain's flag of the White Regiment of
the London Trained Bands, 1643. *Right,* Second Captain's
Guidon of the London Dragoons, 1643

shoulder level, parallel to the ground, and himself charged his
attackers.

ARMS, 1600 to 1660

The wheel-lock was still used by some cavalry until after the Restoration (1660) when the Horse Guards of Charles II were issued
with pistols of this type. The seventeenth-century wheel-lock
pistol was a lighter and more elegant affair than its predecessor.
Writers of the time complained that the wheel-lock was too complicated, easily broken, and tended to jam if left wound for any
length of time. It was difficult to repair when broken, and expensive to buy. Robert Ward's *Animadversions of Warre,* written in
1639, describes the drill for wheel-lock pistols, but his instructions
for the carbines show that the lock is a flintlock with separate pan-
cover and steel with a hook working on the back of the cock as a
safety catch. Other drillbooks show that the flintlock with pan-cover
and steel in one piece was the normal lock for cavalry weapons
during the Civil Wars. Loading was either by means of a powder
horn or by means of paper cartridges. The pistol was fired with the
lock held uppermost so that the powder in the pan was kept
against the touch-hole.

Officers carried more expensive pistols of this type, occasionally
with rifled barrels or able to fire more than one shot. Pistols with
revolving chambers, the forerunners of the modern revolver,

206

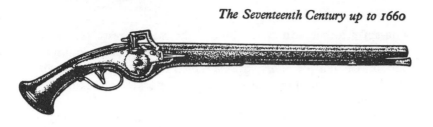

Wheel-lock cavalry pistol, Dutch, about 1650

although rare, were already in use. In 1658 the Danish Life Guards were issued with magazine repeating guns, and a carbine working on the same principle was made by Harman Barne, Prince Rupert's gunsmith, before 1661. Airguns were already in use and one was bought in the Netherlands for an attempt to assassinate Cromwell.

The muskets of the infantry now had triangular butts which begin to look more like modern guns. These were rested against the shoulder when firing. The long sear-lever was replaced by a short curved trigger, like that on a modern gun, which was enclosed for safety in a trigger guard. The barrel was about four and a half foot long at the beginning of the century and as short as three and a half foot at the outbreak of the Civil War.

Since the musketeers were still dependent on their pikemen to protect them from cavalry, efforts were made to turn the musketeers into pikemen. At first this was sometimes done by adding a

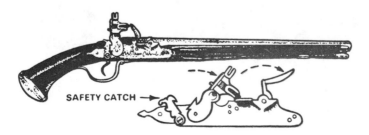

SAFETY CATCH →

English flintlock cavalry pistol, about 1650. The pan-cover and steel in one piece long spike to one arm of the fork of the musket-rest. This was found to be unsatisfactory, and, about ten years after the restoration of Charles II, short knives, called 'byonetts' (bayonets), which could be fixed into the muzzle of the musket, were issued to some regiments.

Just before the Civil War began, a pair of wheel-lock pistols with their tools cost £2 16s. and sixpence for holsters; a wheel-lock carbine cost £1 10s. and one shilling for the shoulder-belt to hang it on; flintlock pistols were £2 5s. a pair and a flintlock carbine £1 2s.; the musket cost from 18s. 6d. to 16s. 6d. The size of the barrels was now made uniform. All pistols and carbines in the Royal Service fired a lead ball weighing $\frac{1}{24}$ of a pound, while the musket fired one of $\frac{1}{12}$ of a pound.

By the Civil War the sword of the cavalry had a relatively broad cutting blade, usually with several flutes, and a basket hilt to protect the hand. That of the infantry was usually a cheaper weapon with two shell-guards on either side of the blade, a short curled rear-guard, and a knuckle-guard. A more elegant version of this was carried by officers, often with a silver hilt or one of chiselled steel.

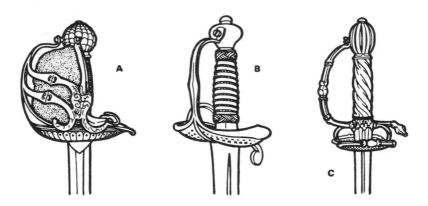

Mid seventeenth-century swords; A cavalry, B infantry, C officers

Under the influence of the simplified French school of fencing, the civilian sword became lighter, shorter, and more manageable. Complicated guards were no longer necessary since the system of swordsmanship was more efficient in giving protection. The typical civilian sword of the middle of the century had a short crossguard with a small circular guard in front of it, or two oval shellguards, one on each side of the blade. Blades as short as thirty-two inches were again in use.

ARMOUR, 1600 to 1660

The full armour of the seventeenth century, although rarely worn, did not differ much from that of the late sixteenth century. The 'peascod' breast was replaced by a much flatter one of broader and shorter form. The tassets, whether the square ones for infantry or the longer laminated ones of the cavalry, were now usually attached direct to the flange at the bottom of the breast. The shoulder defences, since the lance was no longer used, were made the same shape for each side. Good quality armours had additional bullet-proof reinforcing breasts to wear over the other one. At Greenwich armours for the court were still made with additional reinforces for the tilt as before. The locking gauntlet was, however, no longer used for the mounted combat with swords. The foot combat with pike over a barrier continued to be popular. The contestants wore armour only above the waist since the barrier was high enough to protect them below this point.

The tournament was slowly being given up, to be replaced with a sort of mounted ballet, called the 'Carousel', with the riders in fancy dress disguised as Persians, Red Indians, or Romans. This sometimes included running with a lance at a mock contestant, such as a dummy Moor, or attempting to carry off on the point of a light lance a small ring hanging down on a cord over the lists.

TACTICS, 1600 to 1660

The tactics employed by each side in the Civil War were very similar. For instance, at Naseby (1645) both armies were drawn up

209

in a double line of foot regiments, each regiment consisting of a central block of pikemen with two wings of musketeers. In the gaps between two regiments were placed two field-guns coming under the Colonel's command (if there was time it was customary to dig these guns in). On the flanks of the army stood the regiments of horse, also in two lines, each regiment consisting of a number of troops or squadrons.

In 1600 the infantry were normally drawn up in ten ranks, each of which fired in turn, but Gustavus Adolphus, King of Sweden, had trained his men to load and fire faster. Musketeers could now be drawn up in only six ranks and taught to fire three ranks at a time, the front one kneeling, the second row stooping, the third row standing. After they had fired, the rear three ranks took their place and fired while the original front ranks reloaded. In attack they fired two smashing volleys and charged at 'push of pike and butt end of musket'. The heavy iron-shod butt of a clubbed musket was, no doubt, a better weapon than a musketeer's cheap sword. If they were attacked by cavalry the pikemen formed a square, thrusting their pikes out between the musketeers who were drawn up in two ranks outside the square. As soon as the cavalry came within twenty yards the musketeers fired volleys by alternate ranks. These were the tactics used in the Civil War and Cromwell's continental campaigns.

In the drill-books written immediately before the Civil War, the cavalry were to be drawn up in six ranks just out of range of the enemy. Each rank in turn trotted forward, fired its pistols, and trotted back to reload. They only charged when the enemy's ranks were thinned and broken by casualties. At the Battle of Edgehill Prince Rupert, having drawn up his horse in only three ranks in the new Swedish fashion, completely demoralised the Parliamentary horse by trotting forward according to the drillbook and then, suddenly, charging. His enemies, who awaited his charge at the halt, turned at the last moment and fled.

The individual troops charged at intervals of one hundred paces, and the men rode as close to each other as possible. The knee of the left-hand man was locked in behind the knee of the man on his right, whose other knee would be behind that of the man on his right . . . and so on. Thus the troop became a solid missile without gaps through which the enemy could break and, most important, the horses could not turn away.

The early successes of the King's party seem to have been due to a number of factors. Firstly, although there was no standing army to protect the King, he was able to call upon the only first-rate cavalry commander available, his nephew Prince Rupert of the Rhine, and place him in command of a large body of horse drawn from the West Country gentry and their servants. In contrast, Cromwell described Essex's cavalry as made up of 'old decayed serving-men tapsters [i.e. barmen] and such kind of fellows'. Secondly, in Sir Ralph Hopton and his Cornishmen the King had a force of infantry with not only steadiness under fire but considerable dash in hand-to-hand fighting. Thirdly, the numerous small Parliamentary armies, each answering to the committee of the area in which they had been raised, were unable to combine or act together on any concrete plan. Organisation was usually very bad: on one occasion the citizens of London had to send out their Sunday lunches to feed the unfortunate trained band men at Turnham Green.

The turn of the tide came because Parliament had the concentrated wealth of London and its economic and commercial experience behind it. Parliament also had control of the Navy which the King had built and organised in spite of the stiffest opposition from Parliament. Command of the sea meant that they could deny supplies and munitions to the King; the wealth of the City allowed them to purchase their own supplies abroad and to pay their men regularly. The King could not afford regular payment to the volunteers who made up the greater part of his forces, and who had a strong tendency to slip away at harvest and seed-time. On the other hand, the regularly paid forces of Parliament were very largely townsmen with less incentive to desert; at the beginning of the war their best infantry regiments were the trained bands of London. These men alone stood up to Rupert's cavalry at the first Battle of Newbury after their own horsemen had fled;

'. . . they stood as a bulwark and rampire to defend the rest . . .'
The Royal armies had to rely largely on plunder for their supplies,
thus making themselves very unpopular in the local countryside,
while their opponents at least tried to pay for all they needed.

In the end, in order to have an army free from control of the
county committees, Parliament raised England's first standing
army, 'The New Model Army', consisting of eleven regiments of
horse, each of 600 men; twelve regiments of foot, each of 1,200
men; 1,000 dragoons; and a powerful train of artillery guarded by
two companies of 'firelocks'. (Firelocks, in this case probably
meaning flintlocks or snaphaunces, were much preferred for the
men guarding the guns, since there was the danger of a spark from
a matchlock falling into a barrel of gunpowder and blowing up a
gun or ammunition wagon.) The success of the New Model Army
was largely due to the strict discipline of the men and their dedi-
cation to the cause. Whereas even Prince Rupert could not control
his cavalry once they had charged, the troopers of the New Model
Army, used perhaps to the sterner discipline of their church,
rallied after dispersing the Royalist horse and fell upon the exposed flank of the infantry.

Although the illustrations of Prince Maurice's soldiers in 1607
show each one in different dress, the paintings of Gustavus Adolphus's colonels with their regiments drawn up behind them show
all the privates of each regiment wearing the same. Already in
Charles I's campaigns against the Scots (1639–41) some of his
regiments were uniformly dressed. During the Civil War each
colonel dressed his regiment in a uniform but there was, at first, no
dominant colour; the Marquis of Newcastle's Royalist regiment
had white coats. The Parliamentary regiments were also gaily
coloured; Lord Brooke's wore purple, Lord Saye's blue, Colonel
John Hampden's green. Red was, however, a popular colour and
was worn both by the Royal Life Guards and by many Parliamentary regiments, particularly those of East Anglia, each regiment
being distinguished by the colour of its cuffs and linings. Perhaps
because it was largely made up of these East Anglian regiments,
the New Model Army was dressed in red coats, and from that time

on until the nineteenth century the British soldier was a 'red-coat'.

The absence of a distinctive colour for each army made it necessary to wear a distinguishing sign, called a field-mark, to tell friend from foe. At Edgehill the forces of Parliament wore orange scarves, while those of the King wore red ones. At Marston Moor, when cut off among the enemy, Sir Thomas Fairfax was able to ride back to his own lines by merely removing his field-mark, on that occasion a white handkerchief worn in the hat, when he became indistinguishable from a Royalist. In addition to this mark a field-word was given out, which was shouted to identify troops in hand-to-hand fighting: at Naseby, Fairfax's word was 'God our Strength'.

ARTILLERY AND FORTIFICATIONS, 1600 to 1660

The names of guns now mean something fairly definite, and from descriptions of captured guns and references to cannon balls in stores we know the more common sizes of guns used in the Civil War.

The field-train was made up of demi-culverins, that is, guns of $4\frac{1}{2}$-inch calibre firing balls of 9 to 12 pounds over a range of 350 to 2,000 yards; sakers of $3\frac{3}{4}$ inch firing a ball of $5\frac{1}{4}$ pounds over a range of 300 to 1,500 yards; minions of $3\frac{1}{4}$ inch firing a ball of $3\frac{1}{4}$ pounds over a range of 280 to 1,400 yards. The smallest pieces often fired not ball but a quantity of smaller bullets at each discharge. Seventeenth-century guns look very like late sixteenth-century ones but usually have rather shorter barrels. The Scots army, in particular, used light leather guns copied from those used by Gustavus Adolphus. They consisted of a metal tube bound with wire or cord and covered in leather. They were light enough to be transported by one horse but sufficiently strong to be discharged a number of times without bursting. The siege guns seem to have been mostly cannons of seven, that is of seven-inch calibre firing a ball of about 40 pounds, and demi-cannons, 6-inch guns firing a 24-pound ball. The range of both of these would be about 1,700

213

yards. The siege-train included mortars, very short guns which fired a large shell high in the air so as to pass over fortifications. The shells were iron balls full of powder with a short length of burning fuse so that they exploded on, or shortly after, landing.

The gun crew usually consisted of three men: the gunner, his mate, and a helper. The gun was loaded with powder by means of a long ladle, a wad was pushed down on top of that and a ball loaded and thrust home by means of a gun ram. The touch-hole was filled with powder from a powder horn, and the gun was then aimed by the gunner who lay on the trail of the carriage and directed the crew, who pointed the gun with the help of crowbars. It was then fired by means of a piece of slow-match held in the clamp on the end of a long stick, called a 'linstock'. Before loading again, the gun would be swabbed out to extinguish any glowing embers still inside.

Guns were drawn by either horses or oxen: the larger pieces might require seven yoke (i.e. pairs) of oxen or twelve horses, and others would be needed to pull the ammunition carts.

A great number of sieges took place in the Civil War because most of the Royalist gentry defended their houses for the King. When the Parliamentary forces attacked with artillery, the ordinary country mansion, even when surrounded with hastily constructed earthworks, rarely held out for long. The gallant defence of Basing House near Reading by the old Marquis of Winchester for two years is a classic exception. Few English castles had any of the latest fortifications and they fared little better in the face of modern artillery than did the great houses, and once they were captured they were knocked down, blown up, or undermined so that they could not be regarrisoned.

Where artillery was lacking or ineffective, more primitive methods were adopted, assault being preferred with faggots to fill up the moat, scaling ladders to climb the walls, and grenades to hurl in at the windows. If this failed, mining or starvation could be tried, with lines of trenches, palisades, and forts surrounding the house or town. The garrison which had failed to surrender when summoned could expect no quarter when their enemy broke

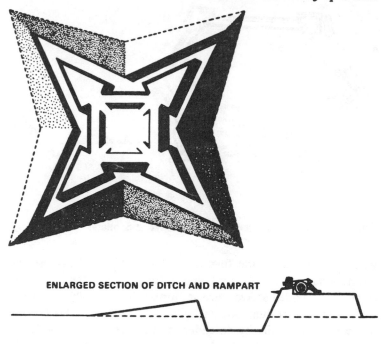

ENLARGED SECTION OF DITCH AND RAMPART

Plan of an isolated artillery fort of the Civil War

in to sack the place; the sack of Drogheda by Cromwell is a by-word for bloodshed in Ireland but many smaller massacres made the war more horrible at home.

The sudden outbreak of the Civil War found both sides unprepared with fortifications, and the majority of those used during the war were hurriedly constructed earthworks faced with wood in place of the usual stone. The plan of isolated forts was usually square or five-sided with, at each corner, large pointed bastions, diamond-shaped in plan. The walls consisted of earthworks of no great height but of immense thickness, formed as gun platforms with a low parapet and a slight slope towards the field. On the outer side of the ditch was an earth bank sloping very gradually towards the field so that it could be swept by gunfire from the

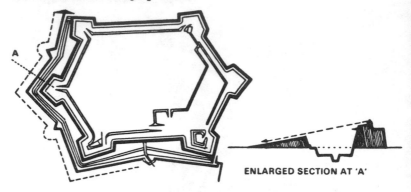

ENLARGED SECTION AT 'A'

Plan of the Cromwellian garrison fort at Ayr in Scotland

walls, at the same time forming a low outer wall against the enemy's cannon shot. Just below the level of the parapet a series of pointed wooden stakes were set jutting horizontally out of the wall to prevent scaling ladders being set against it. This type of fort was used equally by defenders and attackers. In some cases, towns were surrounded by a number of these forts, or with a series of bastions linked by a low earth bank and ditch or by a full-size earth wall, or with a combination of bastioned wall and out-lying forts. The besiegers sometimes surrounded the town with similar defences facing inwards to prevent any attempt to break out. In the absence of complete batteries, guns were defended by huge wickerwork baskets filled with earth.

When the main war was over, the Cromwellian conquest of Ireland and Scotland made garrison forts essential to hold down the conquered populace. The ruins of some of these remain, and many plans made during or after their building. They differ from the forts of the actual Civil War only in being stone-faced. A wooden bridge, with a drawbridge on the inner end, crossed the moat or ditch, and the entrance was through a long vaulted pas-sage. Inside were regularly arranged buildings, officers' quarters, barracks, armoury, stables, and storehouses.

216

Appendix

THE MAKING OF AN ARMOUR

The raw material for armour was iron, and the great manufacturing centres were in the iron-bearing districts of north Italy and south Germany. Each area not only had its own style but a different form of organisation. In Italy, where, from the fourteenth century, large commercial companies in the modern style were common, the great family of armourers, the Missaglia, built up a huge company employing many specialist craftsmen, with agents in the great trading centres abroad. They were able to turn out hundreds of armours a year. Many Milanese armourers settled abroad and were to be found working at Tours for the French court, and in England and Flanders.

In northern lands the medieval guild system kept a firm hold on craftsmen down to the Industrial Revolution. Armourers in the great German centres, such as Augsburg, Landshut, Nuremberg, and Innsbruck, worked in small workshops and employed only a few craftsmen and apprentices. However, an order for 1,000 footmen's armours sent to the Armourers' Guild at Nuremberg, where they specialised in armours for ordinary soldiers, would soon have been completed because of the large number of small workshops there.

Unless a man ordered an armour 'off-the-peg' he would be carefully measured to ensure a good fit. If he lived far away he might send his jacket or a wax-cast of his legs to the armourer. The iron arrived at the workshop in the form of rough billets from the furnace. First, this lump would have to be flattened into a rather thick plate with very heavy sledge hammers to bring it down to a workable thickness. Then the individual plates of the armour were beaten out of the pieces of the flattened billet, and variously shaped hammers were used to work the metal over a variety of steel stakes fixed in the top of the anvil. Although the metal was worked cold, it required frequent annealing (i.e. softening) in the furnace at the back of the shop. Great care was taken to see that the metal was thickest at the front of the head and body, and on the left side, which was the side turned towards an enemy. The edges were shaped by means of a huge pair of shears set in a heavy log to keep them steady. The edges of parts which were going to form the outer edge of a defence were stiffened by rolling them round a wire, to form a stop-rib to prevent a weapon glancing off the edge into a vital part and to make the edge less liable to damage. Each piece was marked inside with an identification mark indicating its relative position in the armour.

Although, at first, probably all the hammerwork was done by hand, certainly by the sixteenth century great water-driven hammers were in use, and by the seventeenth century rolling mills making sheet metal were employed for the manufacture of munition armour.

The pieces were now black from the fire, dimpled all over from the hammer blows, and rough at the edges. The pieces were fitted together temporarily, and the edges were filed to the correct shape, before being given to the polishers, who smoothed the outside and polished them mirror-bright on swiftly rotating grindstones driven by hand or by horses. The pieces then went back to the master armourer who assembled them in the right order. The plates were attached to each other by means of rivets loosely closed so that the pieces were free to move. The lames overlapped like the tail of a lobster or a wasp, and fitted tightly enough to prevent gaps appearing when fully flexed. To make sure, however, each plate was riveted to a leather strap running along the axis of the defence on the inside. As far as possible, plates were made to overlap away from the expected point of attack so that they would shed a weapon, like roof slates shedding the rain. Brass hinges were riveted on the outside of the plates where necessary but, latterly, internal steel hinges were used as being less likely to be damaged in action. Where it was necessary to open a defence to put it on, it was, at first, usually closed by a strap and buckle. In the sixteenth century the outer part was sometimes pierced with a hole which fitted over a staple on the inner piece; the point of a pin, or a hook pivoted on the outer plate, was then placed in the staple, preventing the plates from coming apart.

Once the armour was completed it was fitted with a padded lining in such parts as the helmet, the cuirass, the tassets, and the upper part of the leg. From the middle of the sixteenth century the linings usually show at the edge of the plates as a series of scallops of coloured velvet. These prevented the plates from scratching each other.

From the fourteenth century we begin to read of armours of proof, that is, armour guaranteed as being proof against contemporary weapons. Seventeenth-century armours often have the dent of the testing bullet on the breastplate. The skull of the headpiece and the breastplate could be made thick enough to withstand any weapon, but the defence of the rest of the body and the limbs depended on the plates being very hard on the outside and yet very springy. A weapon striking against these parts either glanced or bounced off.

In the thirteenth century armour was decorated by gilding and painting with heraldic devices. In the following two centuries decoration usually consisted of gilded brass or silver borders riveted to the plates. In the fifteenth century particularly, the armour was often finished a deep blue colour, produced by re-tempering the steel after the polishing. Sometimes decorative designs were made with a sharp punch on the surface of the steel.

In the sixteenth century armour was usually decorated by a method called etching. Part of the decoration was bitten into the surface of the metal with acid, while the part of the plate to be left untouched was protected by paint or wax. The shallow depressions left by the acid were coloured with black paint or with gold.

219

A very few armours were etched and gilt all over, and at least two were also decorated with coloured cold-enamel, a type of paint. Usually, however, the etching is confined to the edges of the plates and a few bands accentuating the shape of the armour. Very wealthy princes bought armours purely for pageants and parades, and in some of these the decoration is hammered up out of the surface. In extreme cases the whole armour is covered with fruit, foliage, monsters, gods, and goddesses in relief, etched, and even inlaid with gold and silver. In some cases, where only parts of the armour were treated like this, they can be converted into real armours for war by means of reinforces covering the embossed pieces in which a weapon point would catch, or by exchanging these parts for plain ones.

In the sixteenth and seventeenth centuries armour was often painted black to save it from rusting, and in the seventeenth century etched decoration was replaced by bands of rather rough, punched work.

Index

(See also list of Contents by Subjects)

Index

Index